Advance Praise for
Digital Photography for Busy Women

"I admit it: I'm a digital dodo! I had over one thousand digital photos stored on a dozen CDs — from just one vacation — and had no idea what to do with them. Laura Oles's book helped me understand how to filter and name the photos so I could easily sort through them in the future, and how to preserve them so my husband and I can enjoy them for years."

—*Linda Formichelli, co-author of* The Renegade Writer: A Totally Unconventional Guide to Freelance Writing Success

"Fun, practical and easy to read, *Digital Photography for Busy Women* takes the stress out of getting up to speed on today's newest digital camera issues. Her helpful tips and practical stories have saved me hours of time. The best part is I am using my camera more often and actually doing more with the picture I take."

—*Lisa Johnson, President of Reach Women and Co-author of* Don't Think Pink: What Really Makes Women Buy — and How to Increase Your Share of This Crucial Market

"This book should accompany every digital camera sold today. If you're going to take pictures and want them to be around to enjoy later, you'll find much of what you need inside these pages."

—*John Larish, Principal, Jonrel Imaging Consultants and author of seven digital photography books.*

"Finally, someone has solved a universal mom problem with easy organizational tips that can really be done! Yes, I would run into a burning house for my family pictures but thanks to Laura Oles, I don't have to!"

—*Maria Bailey Founder, BlueSuitMom.com and host of Mom Talk Radio*

Digital Photography for Busy Women

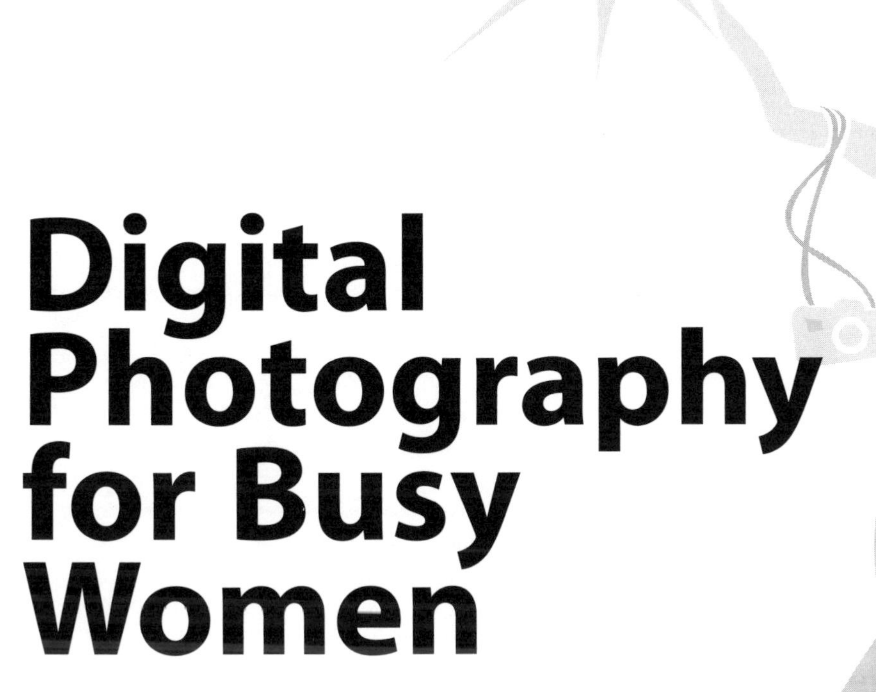

Digital Photography for Busy Women

Laura Oles

Foreword by Kristy Holch

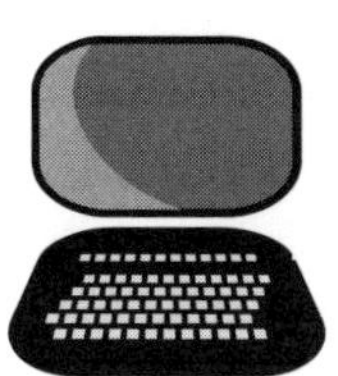

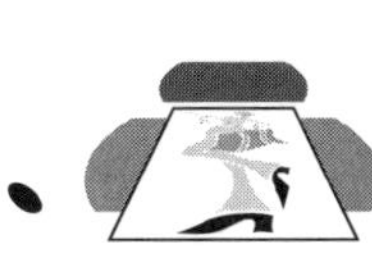

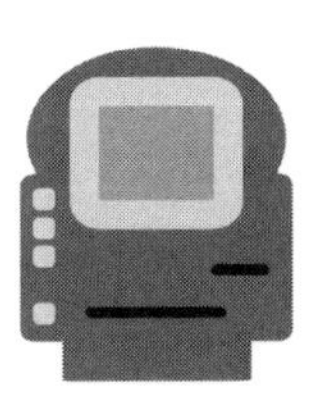

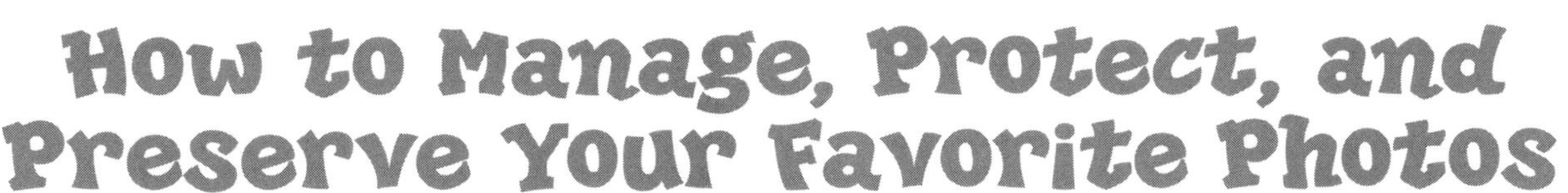

compass
Trade Press
San Marcos, TX

Digital Photography for Busy Women: How to Manage, Protect, and Preserve Your Favorite Photos
by Laura Oles

Published by Compass Trade Press. Available to the trade from all major wholesalers. For information regarding distribution, please contact Compass Trade Press at www.gotdigitalpictures.com.

Cover and interior design by Pneuma Books, LLC. Visit www.pneumabooks.com for more information.

Publisher's Cataloging-in-Publication Data
(*Prepared by The Donohue Group*)

Oles, Laura.
Digital photography for busy women : how to manage, protect, and preserve your favorite photos / Laura Oles ; foreword by Kristy Holch.

p. : ill. ; cm.
ISBN-13: 978-0-9774727-2-7
ISBN-10: 0-9774727-2-8

1. Photography--Digital techniques--Handbooks, manuals, etc. 2. Digital cameras--Handbooks, manuals, etc.
3. Image processing--Digital techniques--
Handbooks, manuals, etc. I. Holch, Kristy. II. Title.

TR267 .O44 2006
775 2006900589

12 11 10 09 08 07 06 6 5 4 3 2 1

For my family—
David, Rachel, Ryan, and Will
I cherish each and every moment

"The distance is nothing; it is only the first step that is difficult."
—Marie Anne du Deffand (1697 – 1780)

"Let your life speak."
—Quaker wisdom

Contents

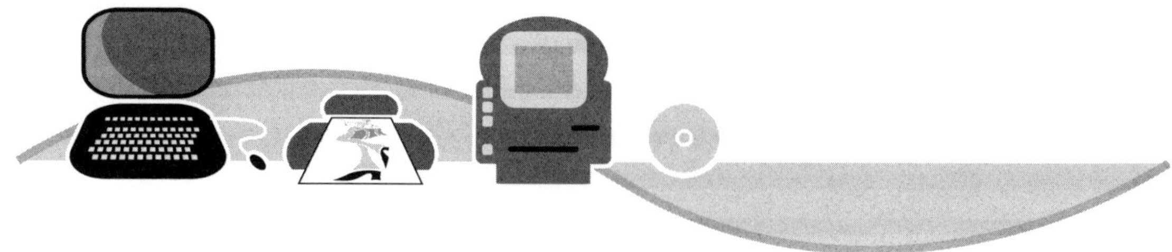

Foreword

As a market research analyst and industry expert, I have tracked the consumer digital photography market since its inception in the early 1990s and championed the rights of consumers as the industry developed. Digital photography has indeed been a boon for consumers, but it has also inadvertently created a potential disaster for consumers — the loss of their photos. In an industry that has already faced several challenges — this is the biggest one yet.

How did this happen? In the early years of the market, all the attention was on the cameras themselves — getting better performance for less cost. The early buyers were hobbyists and tech enthusiasts who could navigate the hurdles of the digital photography process as the kinks were worked out. By 2001, camera features and price points had reached the mainstream, and digital cameras were replacing film cameras because of their incredible advantages. Everyone began buying digital, even the less tech-savvy users and in spite of some bugs still in the system.

Then the focus shifted to the next big problem — photo printing. Consumers could get the pictures in but had trouble getting them out. In fact, we're still in that stage, as retailers vie with home and online printers to give you the best, easiest, and most affordable prints. There are still many improvements to come, but for the most part, photo printing is now easy and accessible to all. The industry will remain focused here for some time, however, because print revenue happens to be a pretty sizeable market — nearly $4 billion a year in the U.S. alone, just for the prints themselves.

Yet there is now an urgent need to shift attention to the third issue for the market — photo preservation and management. The trouble is, neither consumers nor the industry are doing so. For their part, the industry players are struggling with rapid technology evolution, so it's hard for them to give you a reliable and simple way to archive your photos, since the rules keep changing. To complicate matters, there doesn't seem to be much money in it for them; and if they can't profit from it, they can't justify devoting resources to it. For your part, you haven't been clamoring for photo management solutions, and until consumers start making buying decisions based on photo management, the industry will be slow to generate holistic solutions to storage problems.

Why is this such a serious issue? Because only about half of consumers today are saving photos in a way that is considered "safe" for at least the next ten years or so. Sadly, this statistic has remained stuck at 50 percent since we began surveying digital camera users. The safest methods for storing photos today include CD, DVD, online, backup drives, and prints — with redundancy for insurance. Unsafe methods include storing photos only in your PC hard drive or only as non-archival prints. Keeping them on obsolete formats such as discontinued camera storage card media is also risky, since no one will be able to read that media as the years go by. The result is that your photos certainly won't be there in thirty years, maybe not in ten, maybe not even in one.

In fact, even today's "safe" methods aren't the best — media formats evolve, their physical properties can erode, and so on. Perhaps the only maintenance-free digital storage method that is guaranteed to last fifty years (barring flood or fire) is not digital at all — it is archival-quality prints stored behind glass or in an album and not exposed to light. But you can't use prints for email or to quickly whip up a photo calendar. You need digital images as well. Today's digital photos require you to constantly tend them, like maintaining your house or car, or else they will disappear.

Eventually, perhaps in as few as five years, I am sure that the industry will be doing a better job of enforcing standards that will automatically save and catalog all your digital photos, without much effort on your part, making it easy for you to preserve them as the years go by. I anticipate the day when you can tell your camera which photos are your favorites and even add keywords like "Fred and Jane" right after you've taken the picture. Then your camera will automatically put the photos onto your home server, which will back up automatically to another location, and you'll never lift a finger. When it comes time to make the annual photo calendar, you will simply choose from your favorites. If you need to make an anniversary card for your parents, you will call up their best photos from years ago using your keywords (or even facial recognition). If you migrate to a new PC, or if file formats change, or whatever else happens, (and it will happen), your system will know how to keep track of all your photos, organize them, back them up, and keep them accessible to you automatically. Pipe dream? Hopefully not.

But for now, you'll need to invest time in keeping your digital photos alive. Fortunately, Laura Oles freely shares her expertise here to help you do just that. Laura's years in the digital photo industry have given her first-hand exposure to the benefits, as well as the pitfalls, of the digital frontier.

She is an expert not only on the technology but on the plight of busy moms (and others) who have the intelligence but not the time to spend hours figuring out how to safeguard their photos. If you follow her advice, you'll always have access to the pictures you treasure the most.

—Kristy Holch, founder,
InfoTrends Research Group

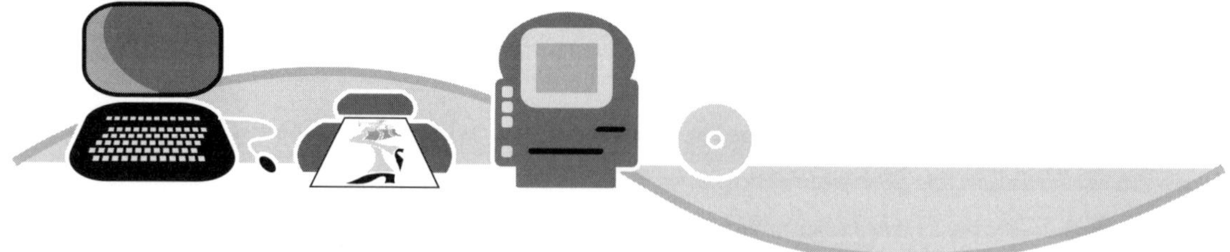

Preface

If your house caught fire and you could only save three possessions, what would they be?

If you're like most people, your photo albums would be at the top of the list. After all, they chronicle your entire life like nothing else — memories, special occasions, and everyday events captured for your enjoyment to return to again and again — they are almost a living history of the most important days of your life. You can close your eyes and envision your daughter's birthday in your mind, but photography records the details your memory may forget — the way she leaned forward to blow out the candles, how the flames created a soft glow around her features, the myriad of smiling faces behind her as she basked in *her* moment. It is photography that keeps the vision alive when your mind no longer can. Photographs, regardless of their form, are one of the most important assets we will ever own.

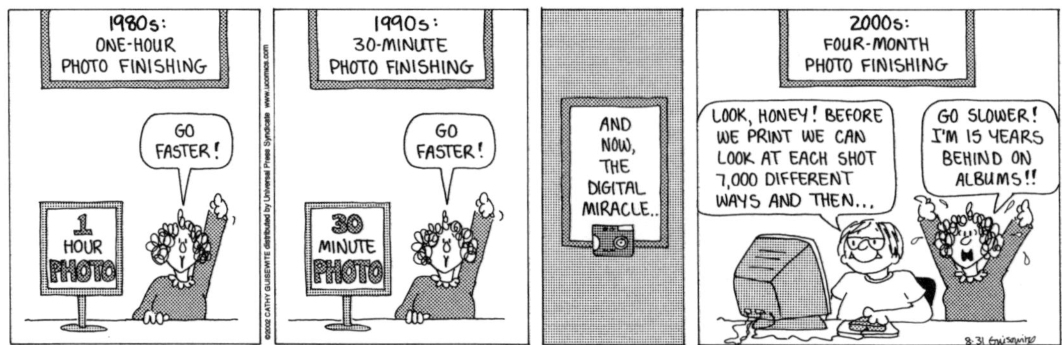

I experienced this on a personal level when we began preparing for a hurricane to hit the Texas coast. We have family living in Houston who found themselves scrambling to secure their homes in preparation for potential damage. My sister-in-law worked diligently to stock up on what she needed, piled her kids in the car, and headed our way in hopes of escaping the hurricane. When we asked her what she had packed in her minivan, she replied, "I've got my kids, some clothes, and my photographs. Everything else can be replaced." Fortunately, her home was spared damage. Still, in that moment of crisis, she quickly decided what was most important, and her pictures — mostly digital — topped the list.

Photographs are an important cornerstone of your family's legacy and a key to understanding past generations. Photography allows us not only to pass down a chronicle of our lives but of the lives of those loved ones that have come before. Those small, yellowed, square pictures put a face to a name when our father tells us of how his mother came to the United States "on the boat" when she was just three years old. Her death before your birth kept us from knowing her intimately, but the pictures give us a sense of who she was, what she loved, and how she lived.

But the scrapbooks of today are nothing like the ones we remember fondly; viewing our precious photos today often means booting up the computer and searching through countless directories for that priceless image. The definition of what constitutes a memory is quite different today than it was a hundred years ago. The methods that produced those precious, vintage photos tucked securely in your grandmother's photo albums are becoming a memory of their own, replaced by new methods of recording our lives. Our most precious moments are now binary code — ones and zeroes intermingling on our hard drives with miscellaneous work memos and a litany of other files. If a fire ravaged those files, we wouldn't miss them, but our photos, however, are another matter. And if your house were immersed in flames or if a natural disaster struck, would you think to grab the CPU in your panic and carry it off to safety? Would there even be time?

The good news is that the odds of your losing your entire picture collection in a house fire are extremely low. The bad news is that you are, according to today's top experts, going to lose some of your favorite photographs in a hard drive crash or other hardware failure. Why? Because all of today's technology ages, much of it poorly, and with age comes instability.

The New York Times article entitled, "E.R. for Hard Drives" tells the story of Ryan Risdal, a father of four, trying to retrieve some photographs to be used at his wife's funeral, only to find that his hard drive had crashed. He told the reporter, "I had six years of digital pictures on the drive, and I hadn't backed up in years."[1] A local company was unable to assist him but sent him to another firm. After being referred to DriveSavers, a company that provides data retrieval for computer equipment, he was extremely grateful to find the entire library could be recovered.

When *The New York Times* asked DriveSavers's co-founder Scott Gaidano about the reliability of hard drives, he stated that they were so untrustworthy that they "should not exist today."[2] And yet we regularly entrust our most important pictures, our favorite music, and our critical financial data to equipment that has proven again and again that it should not be given the sole task of protecting this information.

This book is the result of a personal quest to share what I have learned about digital photo management and preservation over the course of thirteen years in the industry. My interest in this topic grew steadily after I had three children of my own. I'd rather forfeit a winning lottery ticket than lose pictures of my twin boys' first birthday party or my daughter's first horse ride. The mere thought of never having those pictures to enjoy and pass down to my kids is simply heartbreaking.

Analysts, trade reporters, and top consumer electronics executives now cover digital picture management and preservation on a fairly regular basis, and yet it seemed there was little information for today's busy woman on how to better manage her growing library of digital pictures. Part of this lack of information stems from the fact that, although it may seem we've been toting digital cameras forever, they are (on a mass-adoption level) just a few years old. Some early models have a fifteen-year history, but in terms of digital cameras becoming a replacement for film, our silver gadgets are barely teenagers. The imaging industry is beginning to delve deeply into the long-term concerns of how to best protect our picture chronicles for the future, because we've now progressed to the next level of this technology. The picture-quality debate has been decided by consumers, who want to make sure their pictures can be passed down to those who come after us.

Image management and preservation are topics with many layers of complexity. It seemed that the more research and interviews I conducted for this book, the more contradictory information I found. Technology is much like politics in that you can see the benefits and drawbacks of almost any particular issue; the key is deciding which solution is best for your particular needs. While you'll find many guidelines and evaluations in this book, you won't find any absolutes on any particular topic because, quite frankly, what may work for you may not make sense for someone else.

Perhaps nowhere was this issue more evident than in my research on the CD/DVD debate and researching which formats were best for storing digital pictures. Some recommendations I received from experts were based upon which technology would likely live longer in the industry, while other recommendations were predicated upon which were more durable. Still others stated that the biggest issue wasn't how long the CD or DVD would protect your precious pictures but whether you'd remember to retrieve those images and convert them to a new standard before the old equipment became obsolete (just try reading a floppy or a SyQuest disk today to see where this is headed). There is no single perfect answer. Thankfully, there are a number of products to choose from, giving you flexibility in deciding what works for your needs, your time, and your budget.

This book seeks to bring awareness of these important issues and provide some information that will be of value in your quest to leave a legacy. In interviewing many of these experts as well as digital camera-toting women across the country, I explored some of today's most common digital-picture challenges and worked with several well-respected professionals to formulate a strategy designed to give you real solutions — one that fits your busy lifestyle and will give you comfort, knowing that the images that depict the most important moments of your life will be better protected than before you picked up this book.

Time is a funny thing; we all need more and yet we all have the exact same amount. There are twenty-four hours in each day. It is up to each of us to decide how to best use the hours we have. The tips in this book can help you protect one of your most valuable assets and create a system that will save you countless hours in the future.

Close your eyes and envision your most favorite photographs. Relive that memory in great detail and revel in the flood of wonderful emotions that wash over you from that experience.

Now imagine those photographs are lost forever, never again to be viewed and enjoyed.

Please make your pictures a priority. I can't promise that every single step of the way will be a snap, but I can promise that the results will be well worth the effort.

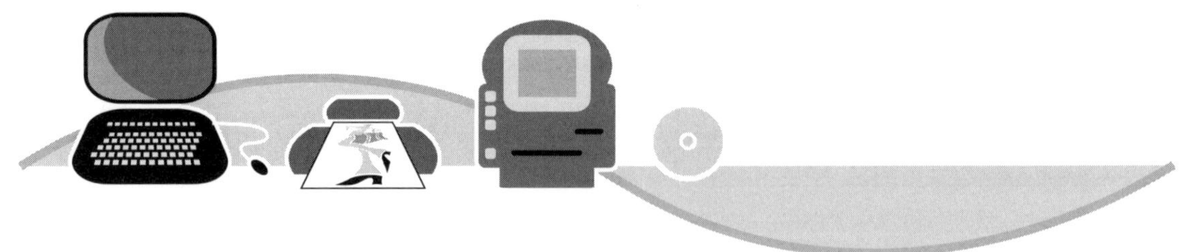

Acknowledgments

This book has been my passion for some time, but it wouldn't exist today without the help, support, and guidance of many people in my life. My husband, David, has served as my sounding board, my partner, and my comic relief. I would also like to thank my mother- and father-in-law, Henry and Marian Oles, who are both accredited professional photographers, because they introduced me to this wonderful industry we call "photo" almost fifteen years ago. It is because of them that I know the difference between an f/stop and a bus stop.

I have been blessed to work with talented graphic designers Brian Taylor, Mike Morris, Lisa Hinson, Silke Aulthaus-Ortiz, and Sarah Handlos and have benefited greatly from their input and support. Editors Nina Taylor, Heather Armstrong, and Rose Ellen Larish tended to my manuscript with a keen eye and a great deal of care.

In working on this book, I conducted countless interviews and worry that if I attempted to list all those that provided their expertise and insight, I would inadvertently forget someone. Suffice it to say, the photo industry is filled with people who love the craft, science, and business of digital photography, and several of them have generously shared their knowledge with me.

One person, John Larish, has been a guiding force and expert resource, and he has probably forgotten more about digital photography than I will ever know. His five decades in the imaging industry are well documented through his books, research, and patents. Most importantly, I consider him a dear friend.

I would like to thank Kristy Holch for providing the Foreword and for the contributions she has made to our industry over the last decade. When our paths first crossed in the mid-1990s, I was instantly impressed with her inquisitiveness and insight. Her reputation speaks for itself.

I would also like to thank my parents — Sharon and John David Konvicka and Dave and Peggy Lemak — for their ongoing support and encouragement. We should all be so fortunate to have such a reserve of kindness in our lives.

My big picture is filled with amazing people. I wish you, the reader, the very same blessing.

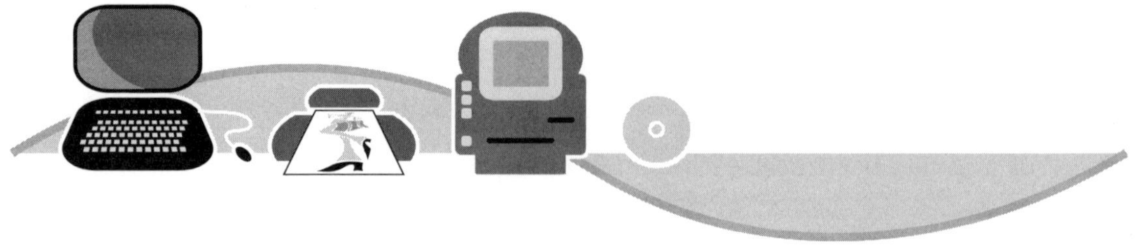

1

The Promise and the Problems

Digital Photography

Maria's days all seemed to run together. She had a pile of laundry taller than Pike's Peak and a department filled with employees anxious after hearing news of a merger. And her home life? She preferred to call the layers of chaos ranging from scattered toys to piles of unfiled paperwork: "evidence of past and current adventures."

Her children were growing out of their clothes almost as soon as she purchased them, and the worry she carried about all the things she still hadn't gotten done nagged her worse than her Aunt Francine. Dry cleaning? Needs to be picked up. Groceries? Always out of something. Oil change for the car? Definitely overdue. Printing photos from digital camera? Don't even go there.

Snapshots

Did You Know?

Ansel Adams, the world-renowned photographer, originally decided to become a concert pianist. It was only after meeting photographer Paul Strand in 1930 that he decided to completely immerse himself in photography. He was also an early consultant for the Polaroid Corporation in the late 1940s.

Maria loved taking pictures and was a regular at her local photo lab when her trusty 35mm camera signaled her roll of film was finished. Once she decided to trade in her film camera for a digital model, she took more pictures than ever, excited about seeing them on the screen and enjoying the fact that she could view them immediately. She just didn't expect to feel so lost when it came to what happened next. She had tons of great memories stored on her hard drive, tucked in various folders marked by a couple of random attempts at organization. She'd remember certain shots she wanted to print to send to her father or to frame for her home, but she could never get those tasks completed.

She loved all the benefits her digital camera provided, but she longed for simpler days when she could just drop off her film and get her pictures. At least with film, she could open up the shoebox and rummage through the pictures until she located the one she wanted.

Why couldn't digital be this way?

When you first hold a digital camera in your hand, admire its sleek design, and imagine all the fabulous moments you'll capture and share with it, you are experiencing some of the best the imaging industry has to offer. Months later, when you're attempting to find that favorite digital picture buried between last year's Christmas newsletter and the downloaded Dilbert comic strip or you're trying to re-size your images to print to your digital photo printer (and find language coming out of your mouth fit for a sailor), you are experiencing some of the worst the imaging industry has to offer. Your experiences — fun and frustrating — are a reflection of what the photo industry has been struggling to tame and explain for the last ten years.

Technological progress is usually considered a good thing. As technology improves, we're supposed to be able to do more, do it better, and do it faster. This progress, in terms of today's computer technology, has delivered countless benefits. But in the arena of digital photography, the picture has proven to be a lot more complicated. For example, being able to take pictures and view them instantly on an LCD screen is a wonderful experience. These digital models deliver far more instant gratification than their film predecessors, but they also require a great deal more from us than our film models ever did.

For the first time in the history of photography, consumers can now control every single aspect of the picture-taking process and create high-quality prints in the comfort of their own homes. "The picture is definitely more complex than it was back in the film era," states Henry Wilhelm, who is considered one of the top, if not the premier, experts on photographic paper permanence. "The downside of having infinite choices, especially with ink-jet printers and paper, is that there are permanence issues that you can't see at the outset. They only manifest over time."[3]

More choices bring more responsibility. We are now completely in charge and accountable for all aspects related to our digital pictures.

This is the irony of digital photography — for all the immediacy and instant gratification it provides, some of the most crucial issues may not reveal themselves for years or even decades. Has our addiction to digital photography's instant gratification fueled a disposable mentality when it comes to chronicling the past for future generations? Maybe we don't care that much about those photographs, but what about those who come after us, longing for a sense of history and an understanding of their roots?

Few of us consider these issues when snapping that picture of our son coated in sand as he gleefully constructs a sand castle on the beach. We are so focused on capturing the moment and making sure the shot is a good one that our attention doesn't extend any further than emailing the photo to family or uploading it to a sharing site. The rest has been taken for granted.

It shouldn't be. The future of those pictures is promised to no one. In fact, it isn't promised at all.

It's hard to fault consumers. The imaging industry is still working to create awareness and the tools necessary to help the picture-taking public easily preserve and protect their digital photo libraries with confidence. There are incredible opportunities to be had for those companies able to identify this issue and then provide elegant and well-designed solutions, and those solutions are coming. The industry is still adjusting to the film-to-digital migration, and this internal chaos remains a factor in addressing the long-term needs of today's picture-taking public.

Take a look behind the digital-photo industry curtain to see how we arrived at this place.

From Craft to Commodity: Pictures, Prescriptions, and Potatoes

The only speed the traditional photo industry once understood is the kind that determines the ISO of film. Up until the mid-nineties, it was a mature market with innovation and change arriving as slowly as a great-grandmother arriving at the finish line of the Boston Marathon. Color film was perfected in the sixties and was made the standard for consumers in the seventies. Polaroid made its mark, giving shutterbugs the ability to watch their pictures develop before their eyes. In the eighties, people found they were able to get their 35mm film processed, and photos printed in just one hour. This change in consumer behavior, created by almost-instant gratification, was the first step in getting moms and dads across America motivated to pick up their cameras and snap shots of their loved ones. Using film was a snap, and now it took just sixty short minutes to see their pictures. Photography became one of America's top hobbies.

> **Snapshots**
>
> **For the Kids — Be Silly**
>
> Try getting your kids to say "fuzzy grilled cheese" or something silly to encourage genuine smiles. Sometimes, those fake plastic grins can be worse than your toddler having his thumb in his mouth.

Film processing as we have known it is a very simple transaction for consumers, but it is actually quite a complicated chemical and optical process. It appears seamless to us because simplicity is critical to getting people to actually take their photos and have them printed. When a busy mom needs to have her film processed, she simply fills out an envelope and checks off how many copies and what print size (3½ x 5 or 4 x 6) she'd like from her film. She can pick them up in an hour, or she can pick them up the next day at a discounted price. She doesn't need to worry about how to handle a slightly under-exposed image, how to eliminate red-eye from a picture, or how to mix photo chemicals so the prints come out perfectly "balanced." That's the photo lab's job. As George Eastman, founder of Eastman Kodak, said, "You take the pictures, and we'll do the rest."

Today's picture takers are much different than their parents in that they have more technology than ever at their fingertips and can handle every aspect of the picture-taking process. But like any technology that brings customer choice and control, there are downsides. Film photography is a sophisticated science made simple for public consumption; digital photography gives consumers more tools than they ever imagined, but they are now tasked with the responsibility of learning every aspect of how to run a personal digital darkroom.

You must learn which ink-jet printer produces the best-quality prints and which has archival inks capable of resisting the fading effects of sun-

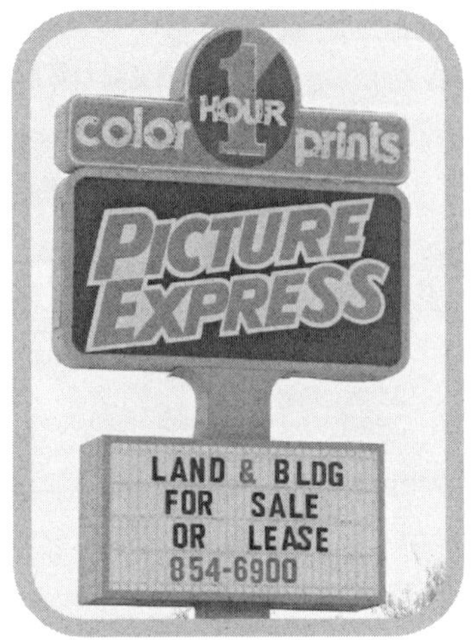

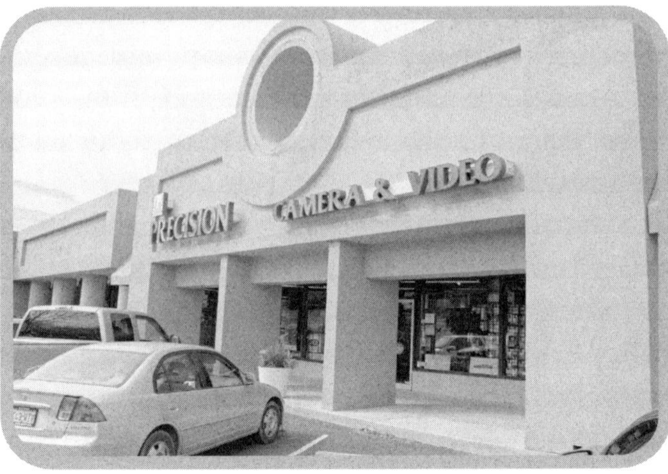

Photos 1A and 1B

The traditional One Hour Photo Lab (left) once so popular in the 1980s has largely gone away as we've transitioned from using film cameras to digital models. Today's photo retailers (right) offer a variety of digital photo products and services as well as workshops and other education for today's busy woman.

light and air. You must learn which digital camera will best fend off obsolescence and then actually learn how to use it. You must learn how to protect your digital pictures, since many will find, only after a heartbreaking loss or computer crash, that digital media is sometimes less dependable than film. You must learn how to marry the digital camera, computer (although some printers bypass this piece of hardware), and printer. And if you want to enhance or correct your photos, you've got tons of options, but the learning curve can be taller than a New York high rise. Now, you take the pictures, and *YOU* do the rest.

Gadget geeks and tech writers aside, do most people really have this kind of time?

Digital photography can be a bit like quicksand in that you don't realize how deep you're in until it's too late. Viewing images on the LCD of a digital camera is a snap; it's the rest of the process that many still find so cumbersome. But once you've embarked upon the digital road, it's difficult to turn back. You're hooked by the instant gratification of viewing your pictures immediately but dismayed to find out that that's exactly where easy street ends.

Fortunately, the consumer electronics industry and the photo industry — still two distinct arenas, although they continue merging together — are beginning to realize the important issues beyond megapixels and price. New innovations are showing up in an effort to help us manage and protect our images; it is still up to us, however, to be aware of these offerings and create a system to guard our most precious memories.

Some frustrated digital shutterbugs are now turning back to their trusty photo labs, longing for the personal attention and expertise they received when they shot with film. Many retailers offer digital photography workshops and educational services designed to help consumers make the most of today's technology. Some retailers even have kiosk cafés where people can sit and relax while printing their digital pictures. The education trend will continue, and soon you'll find more high-quality digital workshops and seminars designed to help you better understand and take advantage of the bevy of features your personal digital darkroom has to offer.

How Did We Get in This Joyful Mess?

In what seemed the time it takes for a camera lens to focus on its target, digital cameras went from an inferior but fun toy to a serious contender to replace film. Buzz about digital cameras had grown steadily since the mid 1990s, although as late as 1999 most executives still discounted their quality. Sure, it was a nifty technology, fun for gadget geeks to play with all through the night when they found themselves without company, but a replacement for film? At the time, it seemed almost impossible to imagine.

It wouldn't take long, though, for the ripples of change to build into a tidal wave. In the mid-to-late-nineties, companies such as Sony promoted

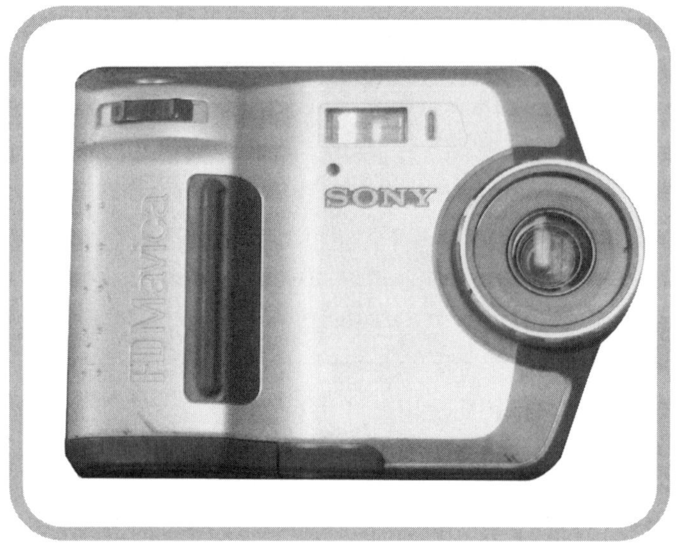

Photo 1C
Many early model digital cameras were not yet considered a solid replacement for film models. While the quality was okay for viewing on a computer screen, they weren't good enough for printing. In just a few years' time, digital cameras were worthy of replacing 35mm film cameras.

their early Mavica digital cameras, which were designed to hold several pictures on a standard 1.44MB floppy disk. The images looked fine on a computer screen, but industry insiders were quick to jump on the fact that the printed images were nowhere close to the quality of a photograph made from 35mm film. While many retailers and reporters discounted these early models, they proved themselves valuable foundations upon which to build. By 1999, digital cameras were hitting the 2 megapixel range — quality sufficient enough for a reasonable 5 x 7 enlargement — and the industry realized it could no longer ignore film's unruly grandchild. While it may be hard to believe, it wasn't until 2002 that the photo industry began offering online digital photo services on a broad basis.

Technology continued to evolve, and the people using digital photography changed. The early adopters — largely men and women who enjoyed technology for the sake of technology — were no longer the majority of those taking digital pictures. The quality, ease of use, and expanding options began attracting film users and soon the majority of digital camera purchases came from (busy) women! In fact, according to the Consumer Electronics Association (CEA), women accounted for the majority of all consumer electronics purchases in 2004, and many experts expect that trend to continue.

> **Snapshots**
>
> **Consider Your Subject!**
> What do you want to highlight in your picture? Is it just the church building or the magnificent sunset behind it? A bit of additional thought will lead to a better photo.

One of the biggest issues that led to having pictures trapped on computers was that the quality of digital cameras evolved far more quickly than the industry expected, so there were few companies able to offer archiving and printing services on a large scale. It was this gap between having more input (digital pictures) than output (being able to get high-quality photographic prints) that fueled the late 1990s gold rush for online digital photofinishing companies. It was almost impossible to go to a retail store and get prints from your digital camera in the year 2000. As a founding team member of a company that introduced one of the very first self-service digital photo kiosk systems, I remember the challenges retail stores faced in trying to fulfill the need for digital prints. Many people turned to online photo service companies or to home ink-jet printers, which have continued to offer increased quality at extremely low prices.

In just a few short years, the entire world of digital photography has changed, and you are at the center of that universe. You have more mind-boggling choices than ever. You have the power *and* you have the responsibility to make sure your pictures are managed, printed, and protected for those who will come after you.

Digital people are indeed different, and their needs are as diverse as the American population. Their use of digital pictures has multiplied exponentially — from simply printing 4 x 6 pictures and dropping them in the mail to mom to emailing, blogging, printing online, storing on CD, using pictures for an online storefront or for an eBay business, creating photo gifts, beaming wirelessly to a PDA, or sending via cell phone.

The Big Picture

Digital pictures are about communication as much as they are about preserving memories, and although the technology we use is far different from the amber-colored rolls of generations past, our primary reasons for taking pictures haven't changed much.

Until the entire process is simple and seamless, we hope this little book will help you enjoy digital photography more, taking comfort in the knowledge that you're actively working to protect your priceless images.

After all, if your house were on fire, what would you grab before running out the door?

- Remember that digital photography brings both joy and responsibility. You are now solely responsible for the safety and longevity of your photographs. Having this understanding is a critical step in preserving your images for a lifetime.

- Close your eyes and envision some of your most favorite photographs. Who do you want them to be passed to in the future, and what are the stories behind them? Gaining this insight will help you as you go through the rest of this book.

- Who do you know that also uses digital photography? Consider starting a small group to provide support and motivation during this process. You'll learn a great deal from them and will also find valuable momentum.

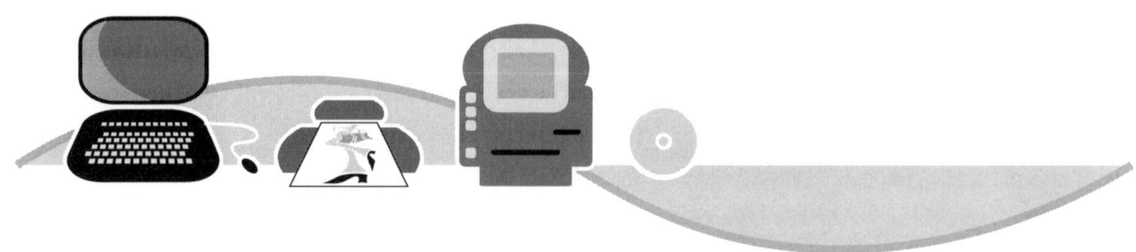

2

FRAME Your Photos

Your Roadmap through the Preservation Proccess

It was *two o'clock in the morning, and the sound of the smoke alarm launched me out of bed like a rocket ship leaving its pad. After my husband, David, confirmed the smoke alarm was merely testing itself (and us), we tried to settle our five-year-old daughter back to sleep. The alarm's piercing siren continued to sound on almost an hourly basis until five that morning. It was only by the grace of a higher power that our two-year-old twin boys slept through the entire night; that fact still stumps us both.*

I remember thinking in my sleepy stupor that the previous night had been more than an annoyance. It had been a warning. Our smoke detectors weren't functioning properly, and this was our chance to verify that this important piece of equipment would be able to alert us in a time of real emergency.

I also remember thinking that our lives were bursting with things to remember. It seems we are inundated with countless details and to-do lists longer than the Tour de France route. With so much to remember, why is it that we often don't make time for the important things, yet we give up precious minutes and hours to minutiae we can't even recall a day or two later? I thought about other women out there, wondering how they kept on top of protecting and preserving their precious photographs with so many other demands on their time.

It was this thought that kept me going the rest of the day.

I share this story with you because, like many of today's busy women, I struggle with a seemingly endless list of things to do and am often frustrated when I can't keep up. On a few occasions, when people see me with my twin boys and my daughter and ask me how I do it, I simply explain that I've just lowered my standards in almost every other area of my life and try to keep my sense of humor. I've realized that there is no getting it all done; I just have to pick what's most important and work hard to keep on track. Some days are better than others. As someone who values organization and a fair amount of structure, the joyful chaos that I call home life is a reminder that I need to pick and choose carefully lest I lose my mind (and my sense of humor).

I am a voracious reader of business books. One of my favorite authors is Jim Collins, author of the bestselling book *Good to Great*, and it turns out that one of his business tenets has served as a foundation in my personal life. Collins promotes a "Stop Doing" list. It seems that part of getting the most important things done in life is knowing what you can leave undone. It's amazing how many things fit into this category. You can read Collins' piece in its entirety at www.jimcollins.com.

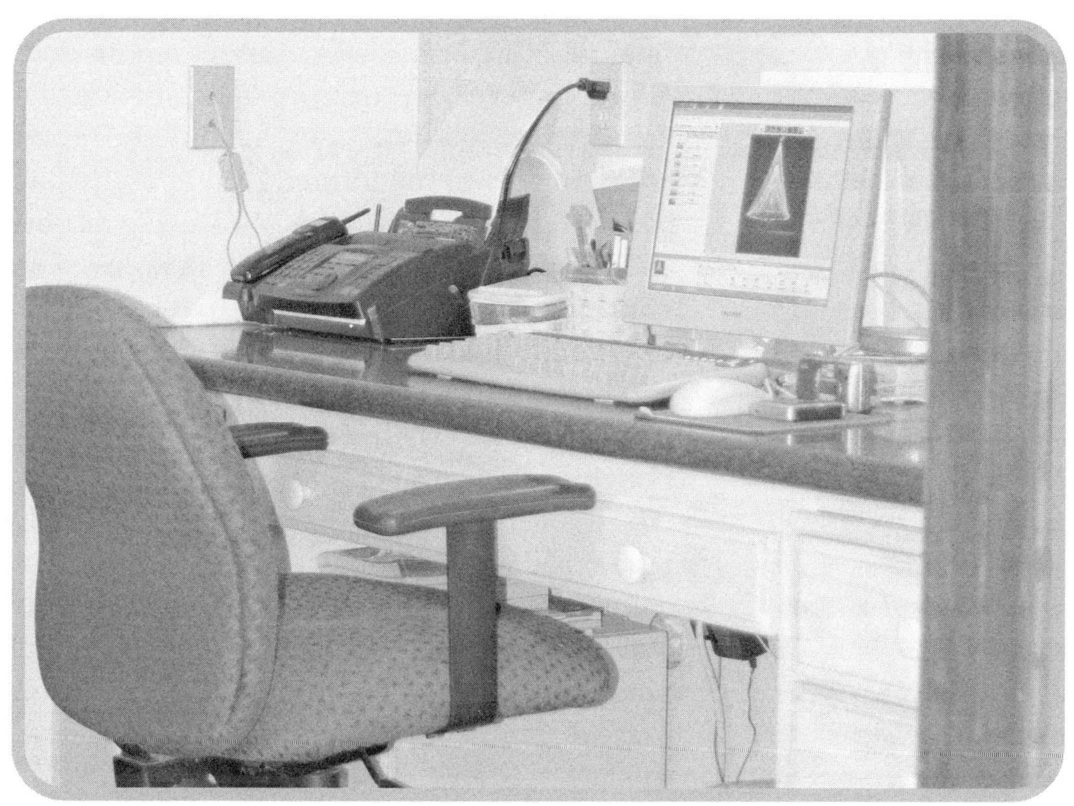

Photo 2A
Like many readers, you may find your home office is located in the kitchen or other central hub of activity in your home. With a little bit of planning and organization, your home office can also serve as your personal digital darkroom.

To-do lists are fabulous and have their place; I am an avid list maker and use them to keep countless details recorded for some form of follow-up. The trick is to make sure that the *really* important things take precedence over less important items that simply make more immediate demands. It's like a ringing telephone; it seems urgent because it's making a loud noise and demanding your attention, but it could just be a telemarketer calling to deliver a monologue regarding a magazine subscription. Things like getting an annual physical and backing up your digital pictures are things you know are important; it's just that they sit quietly in the background waiting for your attention. It's up to you to put those issues at the top of your list and temporarily ignore yet another demand on your time for less-important activities.

I know, I know. Easier said than done. I agree, but I urge you to try.

In an effort to help you better manage your growing library of digital memories, I offer you the FRAME Method™ to serve as a simple road map. Some of my hard-core, tech-intense colleagues may find this a bit too simplistic, but I believe that the reason today's digital photographers are so frustrated with their overflowing hard drives is because they need a launching point, a place to start. I hear the same complaints in interviews with today's busy digital camera-toting women; they need a basic blueprint from which to start so they can get the process moving forward. From that point, there is a wealth of more technical resources available for your review.

Snapshots

The Rule of Thirds
Think of a rectangle with three vertical lines and three horizontal lines. The rule of thirds states that you can add increased focus by making sure your subject is located at any of the four points where the lines intersect. Practicing the rule of thirds is a great way to learn image composition and how to be more creative with your photography.

This method is the result of both experience and research, and the goal is to give digital photographers a straightforward plan that can be implemented with little stress. Appendix C provides a useful checklist to help you implement the FRAME Method™. For ease of use, it can also be downloaded from www.gotdigitalpictures.com.

The FRAME Method™

The FRAME Method™ is a basic foundation to help you manage and protect your digital pictures. Please feel free to experiment or add to it as you wish; you can easily tailor it to your needs.

The FRAME Method™ stands for:

- Filter your pictures
- Reorganize by marking your favorites
- Archive pictures two times with two methods in two locations
- Make a print using archival materials
- Ensure backups are safe with an annual checkup

Step One: Filter Your Pictures

On the surface, this makes sense, but it is surprising to see how often we keep pictures that really aren't that important. I catch myself doing this on occasion, which only causes more work later to go through my libraries and delete pictures that really aren't needed. Because digital photography gives us that instant gratification and allows us to snap away with little concern of running out of space, we tend to snap more often than is necessary.

You're going to have to manage these pictures for years to come, so it's better to be a bit selective either when snapping the photos in the first place (meaning, don't take ten shots of the same thing and keep them indefinitely) as well as deleting pictures before you upload them to your computer. Delete the less-than-stellar pictures off the card first.

I remember a time when I was going through a box full of printed photographs and found several dozen pictures from my wedding. Many of them had been taken by our guests using disposable film cameras. Some of the pictures were fine, but many weren't so great. Still, I had kept all of them because I had paid for the processing and they were photos of people I knew and loved — it didn't seem right to throw away an image of someone I cared about. Maybe it's that little bit of psychology that keeps

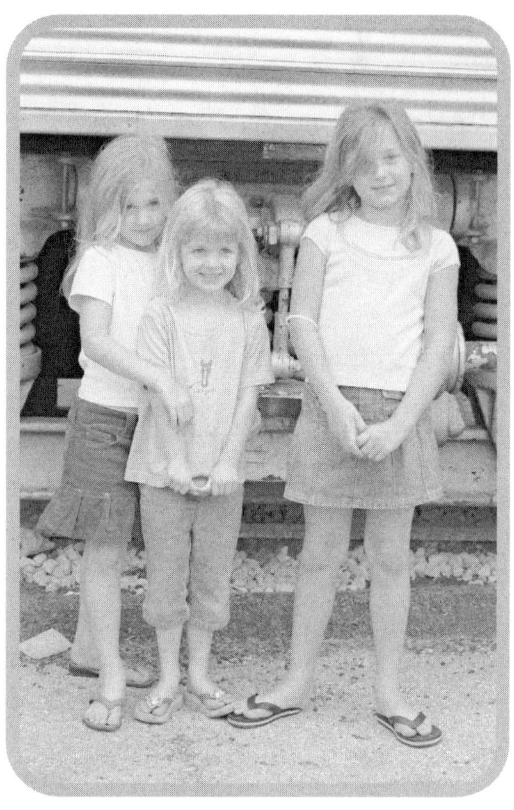

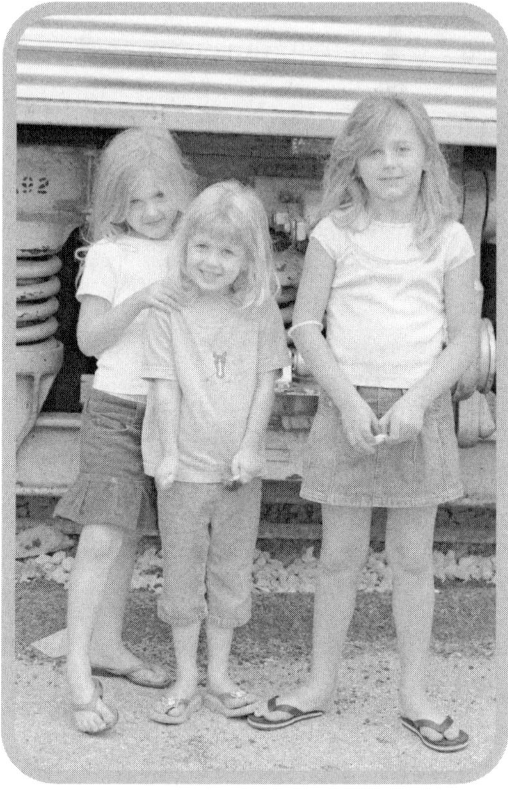

Photos 2B and 2C

Many of us have several images of the same event. Instead of keeping all of them, prune through your images and keep only one or two shots with similar posing. This technique alone will save you a great deal of time down the road.

our hard drives littered with too many pictures, or maybe it's just that we haven't made the time to sit down and delete the extras.

That said, I don't want you to think that your hard drive must only contain shots with everyone looking at the camera. A library full of homogenized pictures isn't the point. In fact, some experts speculate that, in the future, there will be far fewer 'non-posed' pictures and that there is some important back story and history lost by only keeping perfect shots. The pictures must have meaning and value according to your standards. Just apply those standards when deciding what stays and what goes.

Taking this important first step will go a long way in helping you manage your pictures. Think about what you want to hand down to your children and loved ones and which pictures really serve business purposes or other uses. The rest need to go; the physical hard drive space and the mental effort it takes to keep these pictures are too great to be squandered on shots that don't really matter.

Step Two: Reorganize by Marking Your Favorites

"I have almost 125,000 digital images from the last three years, and I can find any one in under a minute." When Peter Krogh, a well-respected professional photographer and board member of the ASMP (American Society of Media Photographers), said this to me, I almost dropped the phone. If he uttered those words to today's average digital camera user, he'd likely be met with disbelief, jealousy, or even a bit of hostility. He insightfully articulates what many consumers feel when they transfer their digital camera images to their computers. "'Am I doing this right? How am I going to find these images? Are they really protected?'"[4]

While most consumers don't have the high-end digital asset management (DAM) software used by today's top-tier photographers, some of today's consumer products will get you going in the right direction and on your way to enjoying your photos rather than being overwhelmed by them.

In order to properly tag your photographs, you'll need to have your image management software selected and installed. Several of today's programs work extremely well and have special tools to help you tag and sort your pictures so that you can find certain ones at a later date. (See "Resources" in appendix B for a more comprehensive listing).

Enjoy taking advantage of all the editing tools as well. Today's category of image management software boasts some wonderfully easy-to-use tools

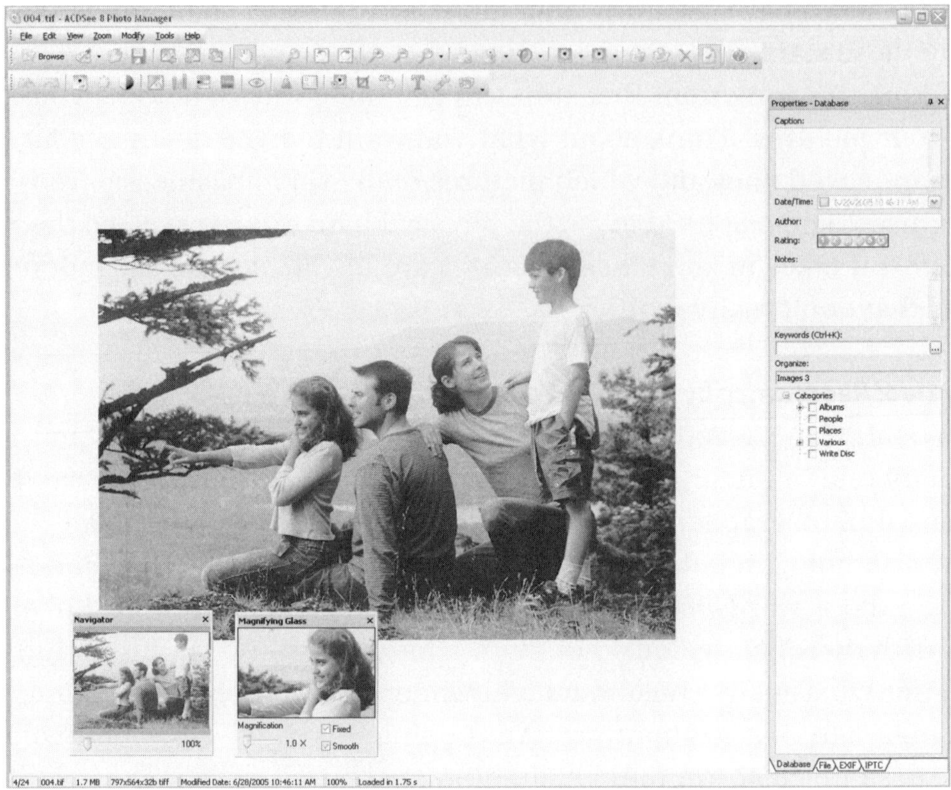

Photo 2D
Marking your favorites in your image management program can help you quickly locate that memorable moment in a sea of other images. Reproduced with permission from ACD Systems.

for red-eye removal, cropping photographs, and color improvement. If you can use the same software for both management and image enhancement, it will streamline the process for you and allow you to build upon your existing knowledge of the software. Once you're comfortable and want to expand, you can grab that Photoshop tome and jump into some advanced image editing.

Remember to use a standard list of terms when creating word tags for your pictures and use all lowercase to keep any caps-sensitive issues at bay. Use a *star* or *favorites* marking features for those pictures that really take your breath away, so you can locate those when the time comes to print or share them.

If you want to keep one picture in multiple albums, some programs will allow you to create a new "instance" of the photo so that it can be found in more than one place without taking up additional space. This is a great way of tracking pictures that you feel fit into more than one category.

Snapshots

Did You Know?
Margaret Bourke-White is considered one of the most famous female photographers, and she was known for her ability to compellingly document some of the most important events of her generation. She was the first Western photographer allowed to enter the Soviet Union in 1930, which later led to publishing *Eyes on Russia*. Her photograph of the Fort Peck Dam was used for *Life* magazine's very first cover.

Step Three: Archive Pictures Two Times with Two Methods in Two Locations

IDC, International Data Corporation, estimates that only 15 percent of home users are actively backing up their hard drives, and that the hard drive is one of the least safe places to keep your pictures long-term. There's nothing wrong with keeping your pictures on your hard drive just as long as you're regularly backing them up and doing so in more than one place.

Using the trusty CD-R or DVD is a great first step in backing up your pictures, and today's prices are so low that this is a great option for those on even the tightest budgets. The second phase of the FRAME backup strategy is to duplicate the archival session a second time with a second method and store it at a different location. For those whose homes are in areas susceptible to severe weather such as flooding, tropical storms, tornadoes, and hurricanes, this is even more critical. It won't help to have all your pictures backed up twice if everything is stored in one place.

One of the most efficient and effective ways to back up your pictures off site is to use an online photo service. There is a difference between photo-sharing and photo-storage sites (see chapter 5 for explanations). Many of today's sharing sites will let you store pictures on their servers, but some require that you order products from them on a regular basis to keep your account active.

You'll find some companies that now specialize in long-term storage of digital photographs, and a little bit of research will help you find the best solution for you. If possible, look at the company and learn as much as you can about their history, their customers, and how long they've been in the business. While there are no guarantees, a little checking will serve you well.

Step Four: Make a Print Using Archival Materials

This step will provide you with not only an additional method of archiving your photographs, it will also bring a new level of satisfaction in regard to your pictures. While we don't print photos nearly as much today as we did with our film cameras, there is still a special satisfaction we feel when holding a printed picture or viewing it in a frame or in a scrapbook as opposed to simply seeing it on our computer screen.

When printing your pictures, it makes sense to pick your most cherished shots. Go through your favorites list in your image management software and use that list to decide which pictures you're going to print. Because you've already marked your favorite shots, deciding which ones to print will be much easier than had you ventured to do this before that task was completed.

If you choose to print your pictures using your own ink-jet printer, remember to verify that you're using archival-quality inks and papers. Follow the printer manufacturer's guidelines to ensure that your pictures will weather time and the elements. Please refer to chapter 6 for additional tips regarding caring for printed photographs.

If you don't want to print your photos at home, you can use an online photo-processing service (maybe the one you've chosen for image storage), or you can take them to your trusted photo shop, drugstore, or supermarket.

Today's photo retailers work extremely hard to provide expertise, quality services, and an experience that you'll enjoy — one that will keep you coming back again. Their experience can be especially useful in the areas of digital-print permanence as they're accustomed to doing their homework to ensure that the printing services they provide to the public will stand up to scrutiny. Essentially, these retailers do much of that work for you and will handle the printing at a competitive price. If a retail experience is not living up to your expectations, find one that will. Don't settle for anything less.

Step Five: Ensure Backups Are Safe with an Annual Checkup

This is a step that many of us will want to skip because we've already been so great about filtering, managing, and backing up our pictures that the thought of going back to check them on a regular basis seems a bit... well... anti-climactic. While it's true that this step may be less involved, you may find it to be the most fun and the one that takes the least amount of time.

Each year, schedule a time where you'll go through and open up your files to verify that they can still be accessed. You can tie it in with spring cleaning, new year's resolutions (in fact, it could be a new year's resolution and would be a lot easier to complete than getting to the gym five days a week), or the start of a season that signals, for you, a fresh start. I'm betting that if you're reading this book, you've already got a calendar system — be it a planner, a PDA, a program on your computer, or a mixture of these time management tools. If you're using an electronic method,

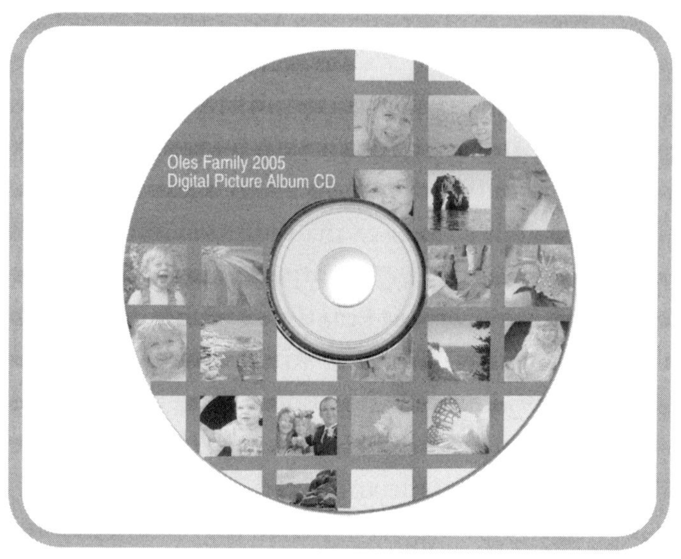

Photo 2E
Take the time each year to open your archive files to make sure the pictures can still be accessed.

schedule an annual appointment with yourself to check your image files, and create the appointment with no end date. Each year, it will remind you and gently nag you to check those pictures. This is an effective strategy and one that people often use to make sure that important issues get the attention they deserve.

A second benefit of visiting those files to verify their safety is the stroll down memory lane you'll take when opening them. It is likely that the pictures you've tucked away on those CDs or on that removable hard drive haven't been viewed in a while, and this exercise will bring back those memories and reward you with a flood of good emotions. It's a chance to relive your kids' early years, your wedding day, your all-girls hiking trip, or your first parachute jump. You may find that this part of the FRAME Method™ encourages you to revisit those images more often, which is one of the greatest benefits of photography — the ability to capture a moment in time and enjoy it endlessly.

If you've stored your pictures with an online service, go through the albums, double check your account settings to verify that all your contact information is current, and consider ordering at least one small item to keep your account active, if required. If you aren't sure of the status or if there has been a policy change, call the company and ask a few questions regarding the safety of your images and inquire about any new developments.

I would also strongly recommend that you create a new, full backup each year. If you find it cumbersome to go through your disks, you may just test a couple of them and not realize that certain files can no longer be opened. By creating a fresh backup annually and then checking it to make sure all is working well, you'll rest better knowing that these pictures have been backed up and protected every year.

> **Snapshots**
>
> **For the Kids — Try Later**
>
> Sometimes we try to take pictures at the most inopportune moments. If the kids are starving or if it's late in the day, give it a shot but don't be discouraged if you can't get unanimous cooperation. A little empathy and tuning into your kids can tell you a great deal about when the best time should be to coordinate a group shot.

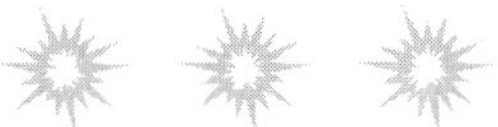

I created the FRAME Method™ to help you form your own methodology for managing, protecting, and preserving your photographs. If this exercise has helped remind you of the immense intangible value of your photographs, I would consider it a success.

The Big Picture

Rather than thinking of this process as another issue that demands your attention, consider how much better you'll feel knowing your pictures are being properly cared for and how much joy and history you'll be preserving for those close to you. All to-do list items are not created equal, and in the list of priorities, consider adding this one and discarding something related to cleaning! Chances are, the dust will still be there. Your pictures? That's another matter.

- In the heavily scheduled and blissfully-filled space that is your life, realize that small steps taken on a regular basis will get your images organized, protected, and preserved. Don't worry about doing everything at once. Just start down the path today and consider creating your own to-do and stop-doing list. Ten years from now, will the time you're spending on all tasks be equally important? Can you fit a bit of time each week into caring for your digital pictures in order to leave a wonderfully rich photographic legacy for those who come after you?

- Use this opportunity to sort through all the digital pictures on your computer. Feel free to delete any pictures that really don't matter or are extremely similar to other shots. This action alone, done on a regular basis, will greatly reduce the number of images you must manage and ensure that the pictures you leave behind are the best ones you have to offer.

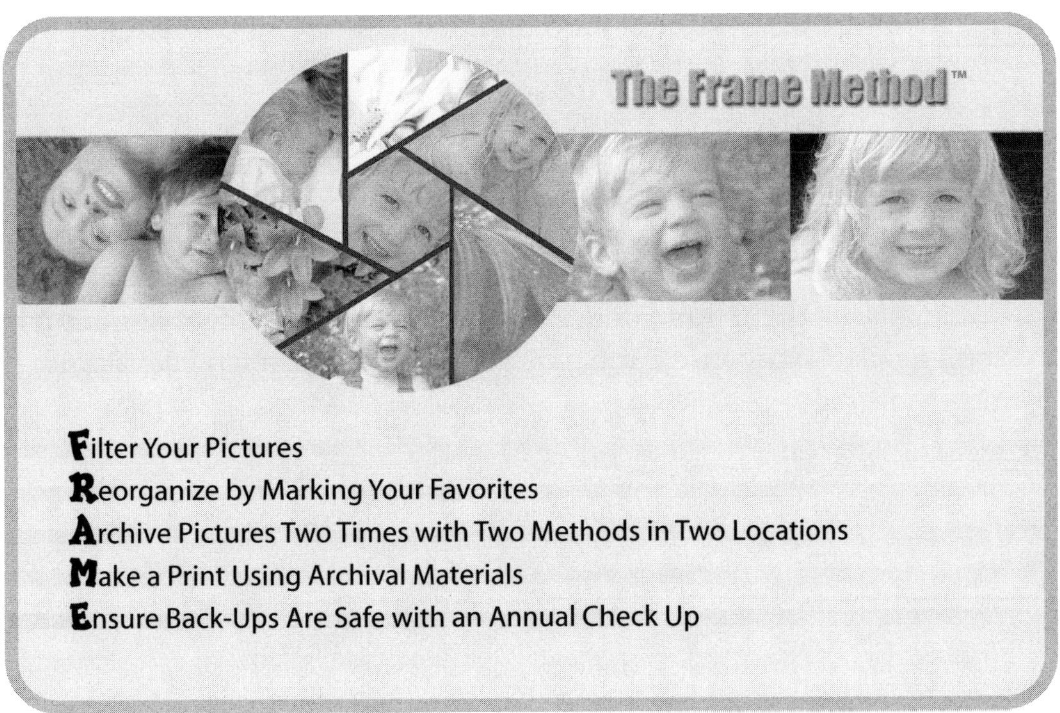

Photo 2F
The FRAME Method™

Take the FRAME Method™ and tailor it to fit your needs and your schedule. It stands for: Filter your pictures, Reorganize by marking your favorites, Archive pictures two times with two methods in two locations, Make a print using archival materials, and Ensure backups are safe with an annual checkup.

- For those who use an electronic calendar system, create a recurring task to check your currently backed up pictures. It may make sense to time it in conjunction with spring cleaning or some other de-cluttering ritual such as a regular donation drive or a garage sale. Use that momentum to get started and continue on a regular basis.

- The more important the data you have, the more often you need to back it up. If you're a writer or a photographer, back up every time you've made substantial progress on a project. For your photography, every time you have a set of pictures you really care about, take the time to back them up in one way or another while you're attention is still focused on the task at hand. Think *download, then back up.*

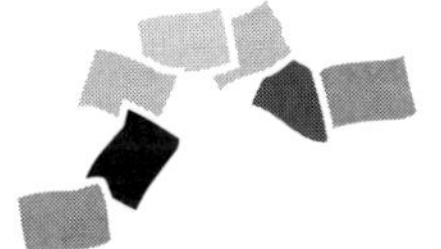

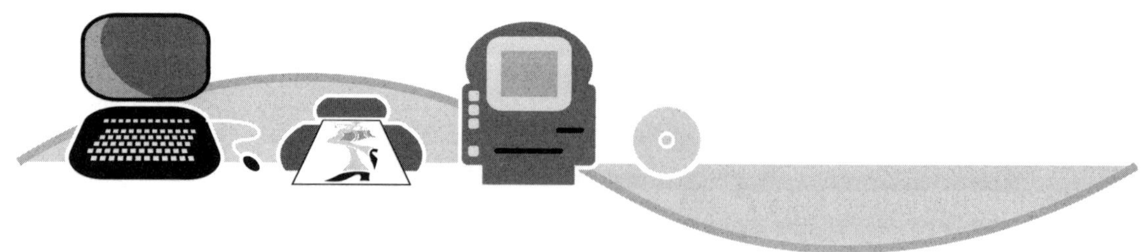

3

Remember Maui?

Manage Your Photos Today to Enjoy Them Tomorrow

"Our digital pictures seem to multiply like rabbits," Anna sighed, as she searched through her hard drive files for the photo her brother had requested. With the family reunion coming up, there had been a frenzy as relatives worked to compile pictures of everyone attending for the reunion picture slide show presentation. Anna's pictures all had cryptic file names like DSC_4533.jpg, and her chest tightened as she continued to wade through the countless files burdening her hard drive.

"Why did I even keep this one?" she said as she surveyed a blurred image of her son moving at what seemed to be the speed of light. No wonder she couldn't find that group shot from their Maui vacation last year; the only pictures she could find were poorly lit or ill-framed.

After another twenty minutes, Anna decided it was time to take a break from her picture-finding expedition. Her stroll down memory lane had quickly turned into an aimless meander through mediocre pictures, and she still didn't have the one she needed.

Think of one of your favorite pictures. If you had to locate it, do you think you could quickly retrieve the image on your computer? If a client asked you for that shot you took last year of their grand opening, could you find it without breaking a sweat? If you needed to put together a slide show for your parents' wedding anniversary or for a family reunion, could you do it without any stress?

If you answered no to any of these questions, you're in good company.

When it comes to digital cameras, it's all too easy to take lots of pictures without any real thought as to whether the picture is one worth keeping. We tend to keep shooting and figure we'll clean up the bad ones later. I'm not one to lecture here; I did the exact thing recently as I tried to get a shot of my three kids together. There are a dozen pictures that aren't worth keeping, and yet, they're all still on my memory card. I'm going to delete them. Really. I just got distracted for a moment. Have you ever seen twin boys scale a fireplace?

The good news is that there are a plethora of good image management programs on the market, so creating a system that will allow you to find what you're looking for is easier than ever.

Delete First, Download Later

There are usually a number of other things going on when we're taking photographs. Maybe we're trying to get a group of people centered in the shot or trying to get all of the kids looking at the camera at the same time (something I believe is about as easy as nailing Jell-O to the wall). We might be trying to manage a client's request for a specific angle or racing against a setting sun so the "perfect shot" isn't lost. Whatever the case, it's likely that there are a number of things demanding your attention. It is often because of this immediate chaos that we tend to take a lot of pictures, many that don't fit our criteria but remain on our camera card anyway.

Regardless of the demands, as soon as you get a free moment, make sure to delete those pictures that aren't up to your standards. Be ruthless in this regard. If you don't think you'll use it, delete it now. While it is tempting to say that you don't have time to filter the pictures right now, remind yourself that these few moments of effort are going to save you a great deal of time, frustration, hard drive space, and media card memory now and later. I did get back to those pictures and delete them; the thought of uploading them to my hard drive and having them clutter things up was motivation enough to make sure the task was complete before I went to bed.

Snapshots

Did You Know?

The word *photography* stems from the Greek words for *light* and *paintbrush* and when put together, means "drawing with light." Photography is, in essence, making pictures by recording specific light patterns.

Another time and memory-saving strategy is to snap and move on. Once you've got the shot and you're happy with it, move on to the next scene. If you really want to take "just one more," make sure that you're happy with the results. If not, go for the delete button!

I'm at the Computer — Now What?

Image Management Programs

There are a few strategies you can implement that will greatly increase your ability to locate your favorite photographs and to manage the burgeoning photo library on your hard drive. The single most important step

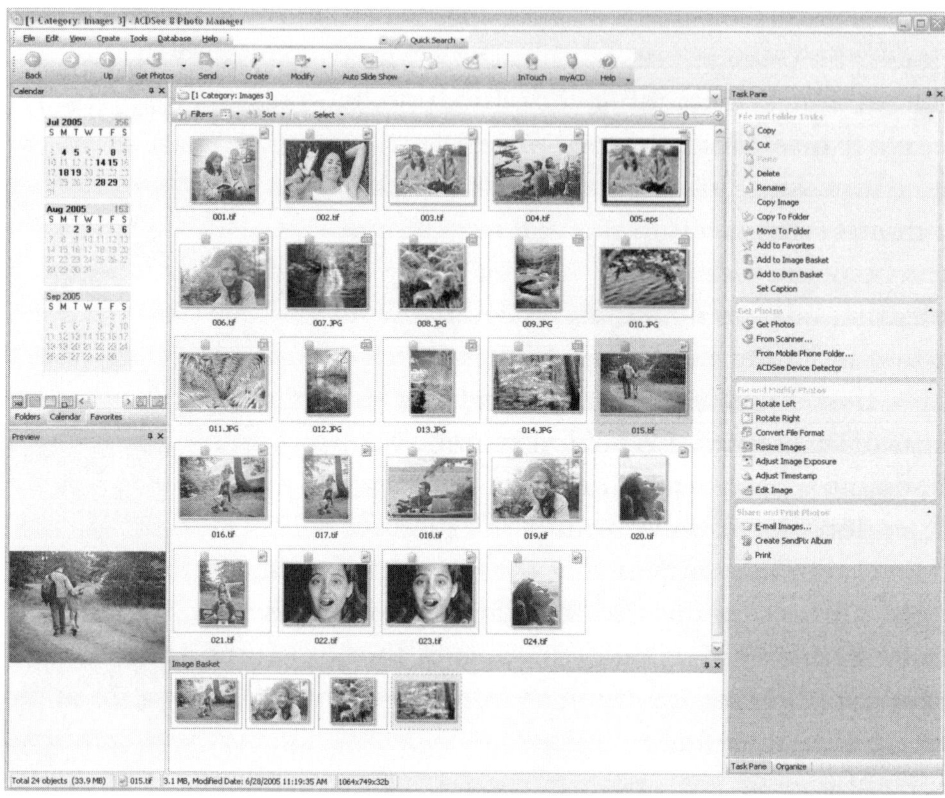

Photo 3A

Using a program such as ACDSee™ 8 can greatly reduce the amount of time you spend searching for your favorite photographs. *Reproduced with permission from ACD Systems.*

you can take when working to manage your pictures is to get a good image management program. While each of these programs has strengths and weaknesses (see the "Resources" section for a listing of some products to evaluate), they have been on the market long enough for their developers to evaluate consumers' needs and to have worked on creating products that make this process far easier on us than in years past. By using an image management program you can:

- Scan your hard drive for all picture files (.jpeg, .tif, and so on) and automatically sort them based upon the data (date/time) embedded in the file (just make sure your camera's time and date are set properly!)

- Create simple naming systems to divide pictures by vacation, season, year, or event

- Mark your favorites so that you can run a special filter of your most favorite shots

- Easily size your photos to send as email attachments

- Post your photos to your blog or website

You don't need to start from scratch when using an image management program. Even if you've got digital photos scattered throughout your hard drive, many of these programs will scour your drive and do much of the initial organizing for you. The experience is almost as satisfying as eating homemade fudge. Many people find that using an image management program helps propel them to better organize and share their photos and gives them a launching point.

Furthermore, if you use a PDA or a camera phone, some of today's image management programs are designed to help integrate the pictures stored on mobile devices. If you have pictures stored on removable media cards, some of these programs can also easily scan for those devices, detecting the pictures and then moving them into the master image library. If you find you've got some great shots on your camera phone and a few lingering on an older media card, these programs can rescue your pictures from the fringes and incorporate them into your comprehensive storage system.

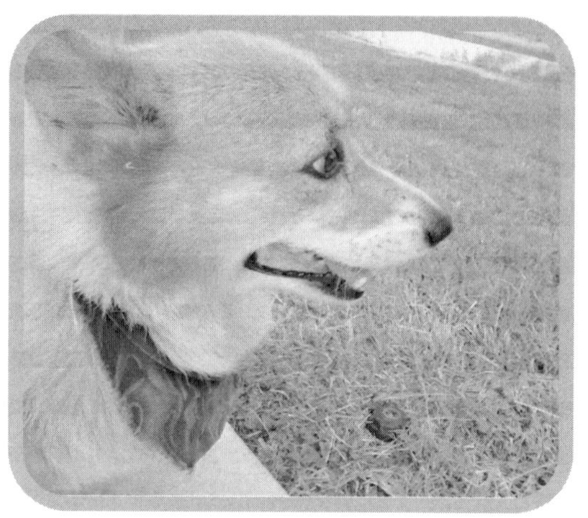
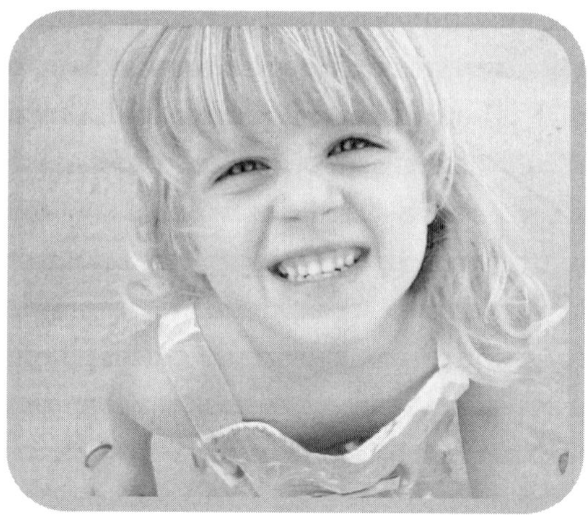

Photos 3B and 3C
When compiling all your digital images, don't forget to include images from your cell phone, your PDA and photographs sent as email attachments.

Today's crop of image management programs offer printing and archiving functions, and these come in handy when you owe printed photos to grandparents or want to make sure your favorite shots are properly backed up.

Some of these programs will allow you to print a contact sheet, which is a sheet of small thumbnail pictures that can be stored with your archive CD. Contact sheets are a wonderful way to quickly assess what is on each CD and can also alert loved ones that important photographs are on those silver discs.

A few of these programs also log information about what image collections have been previously burned to CD (or DVD) — something that is helpful in tracking your archiving activities and can also help you locate images saved on disc.

Some software programs offer another benefit — "batch tools" that let you select a group of pictures that need to be rotated, transferred, or edited. While the tools and functions vary depending on the software program used, taking advantage of a batch process is a good way to help you complete the same function or technique on a group of pictures instead of having to repeat the process multiple times on each photo individually.

Many find that using an image management program is one of the single best investments in getting their pictures sorted, shared, and organized. Most companies offer free trial (and some full) versions of their software, which can be downloaded from their websites, so consider playing with one to see if it meets your needs. If it doesn't, simply uninstall the program and try another. You will want to check the company's 'About Us' section to get a better understanding of how long the company has been in existence, its commitment to the products it creates and other telling bits of information that will help you choose the right product for your needs. Because you'll likely depend on this program for awhile (and will have invested time and effort learning to use it), protect those investments by verifying the company has some solid credentials and deserves your trust.

Experiment, play, and take your time. There are a number of choices available, and once you decide on a program, you'll be amazed at how much easier the rest of this process will be for you.

Using Your My Pictures *Folder*

If you don't want to use an image management program, you can create a simple system using folders and subfolders in your My Pictures folder on your computer system. If you go this route, you'll want to give some thought as to how you're going to group these pictures. For example, you might create a master 2006 folder with subfolders for each month, season, or event so that you can easily import your images into the appropriate places. Some people prefer to organize their folders chronologically while others recall specific events (such as Canada Fishing Trip 2006 or 2005 Ohio Summer Vacation). There is no right answer here, and you can also combine the two options, a strategy we use at our house. We have a year folder (2005) and then a subfolder that shows each month and then subfolders within the month for specific events (e.g., 2005/June/Rachel Birthday Party).

Are you the "photo ambassador," the person assigned to sharing and distributing your family's photos to loved ones? Do you have a special scrapbook in progress? Do you use photography as part of your business for marketing and promotional projects? Do you take photos for clients?

Snapshots

Zoom In!

Many times a photo can be greatly improved by simply moving closer to the subject or zooming in so your subject is well-framed . Don't be afraid to use your zoom (check your camera and use the optical zoom rather than the digital zoom).

Spending a bit of time to devise a strategy based upon your existing and future needs regarding these pictures will help you create an efficient naming and filing system that will allow you to get your hands on a particular shot quickly and efficiently at a later date.

Renaming Your Pictures

For those who wish to get a bit more advanced and are willing to invest more time, consider renaming your pictures. You may want to begin with naming only your most favorite pictures in order to easily find them amongst the hundreds of other shots on your hard drive. Consistency and brevity are important here; create a few key categories, and when adding more, check your existing list first. Renaming pictures can go from being a helpful tool to a tedious task, so if you're unsure, use the "mark favorites" feature of your image management program.

For instance, if you have a group of pictures from a recent vacation, create a short name and then use numbers (Vail_2005_1.jpg, Vail_2005_2.jpg, and so on). You might find that a time or event-based system is preferable to using a person's name. If you run a search and you have used only people's names, you'll have many more pictures to sort through. Also, we tend to remember pictures and events based upon a time or certain situation, so this method may be better for helping you locate those pictures later.

If your photo library is so large that the idea of renaming each picture is about as appealing as having a root canal, you may want to prune your digital files first. If you have five shots of the same people in slightly different poses, pick one or two and then delete the rest. If you do this and would still rather have dental work than rename your photographs, consider adding comments to the EXIF data.

EXIF stands for Exchangeable Image File, and the term refers to certain information recorded by the camera to the digital picture. Some items may include the date and time, whether a flash was used, and exposure details. Many people analyze the EXIF data to better understand the characteristics of an image to determine which camera settings resulted in the best quality pictures. It can also be used as a way to organize and *tag* your pictures.

You could modify the EXIF data to include key words to help identify the photos so that you could search for particular categories later. Most digital camera include some software that will allow you to view EXIF information. If a program or a web browser can read a JPEG file, it should be able to read the EXIF data as well. Applications vary in how they use the data in sorting, so consider trying a free version and playing with the program before committing further time and energy.

That said, there isn't any one right way to create a naming system. If it makes sense to you and works, use it.

Picture Editing Programs

If you could throw a rock into cyberspace, you'd easily hit at least one digital photography editing program. It seems that it was only a few years ago that Photoshop was considered a high-end program reserved for professional graphic artists; now Photoshop is considered a verb, and entire bookstore shelves are dedicated to teaching even the most casual user how to edit their pictures and create masterpieces from the common snapshot.

These programs have a great deal to offer, and today's image management programs now boast many of the most popular features, such as red-eye removal, cropping, color balance, and special effects. It would be unrealistic to tackle this topic in this book because of the sheer depth of material available (check the "Resources" section for some programs to consider), but there is one thing you need to remember when editing a picture with one of these programs — edit a *copy* of the picture and not the original!

When saving a retouched version, make sure to give it a new name (but similar so you can track it). Too many times, people have found the edits they thought they liked don't live up to their expectations or they change their minds later. Sometimes edits look better on the computer screen than they do on the printed photograph. Keeping an untouched original is important when doing any editing to a picture.

There is another reason to hold onto the original file, even if you like the edits and cropping you've completed. Each time a picture is modified and saved, a small amount of image degradation occurs, so if you want to further enhance an image from a quality perspective, you may want to open the original file, re-apply the edits (such as red-eye removal) and then also apply additional edits (such as color adjustment). Just remember to open and save JPEG files with care to keep image deterioration to a minimum.

The Big Picture

The first few steps may be the most difficult, but once you begin, you'll find the rest of the path will be much smoother. Finding a good image management program will help tremendously and will greatly speed up the process. Enjoy this exploration and consider the sense of accomplishment you'll have and how much easier it will be to locate your favorite images once you've put the process in place. I guarantee it will be more satisfying than reorganizing the hall closet.

- Delete any poor pictures immediately. One of the benefits of that LCD screen is being able to make sure that your subject's eyes are open and that you haven't cut off anyone's head. If the picture doesn't make the cut, delete it now and save yourself precious time and hard drive space later.

- Consider using an image management program to help you get those pictures in order. If your hard drive is already filled with photos, it is even more important to begin this process.

- Learn a bit about batch processes to help you streamline your image rotating and other organizing functions.

- For advanced users or enthusiastic organizers, consider rescuing your pictures from cryptic names such as DSC_4332.jpg by creating simple naming groups based upon an event or time period or create different categories and add them to the EXIF data.

- Remember to think about how you intend to use these images down the road. Understanding your needs and goals will guide you in creating a simple system that works for you.

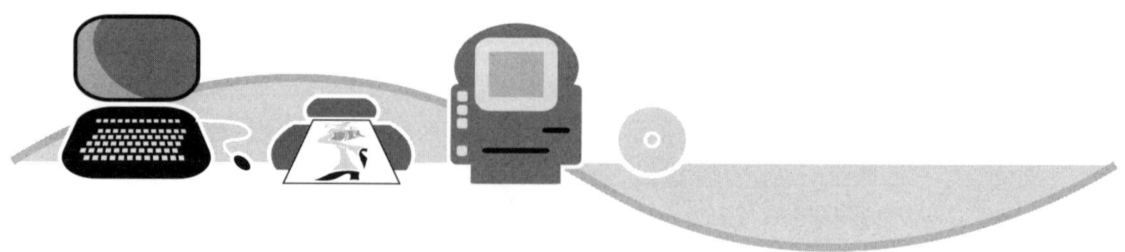

4

The Backup Plan

Hard Drives, CDs, and Camera Cards

Michelle used her digital camera often enough to have it become a regular occupant in her purse. Running her own business meant wearing several hats — sales, marketing, operations, you name it — and the ability to take quality photographs and create marketing materials herself was a great way to keep her costs down. Her one-woman consulting firm kept her juggling more balls than a circus performer, but she loved (almost) every minute of it.

Michelle also enjoyed snapping photos of her niece and nephew and had many photographs just waiting to be delivered to her sister. She just couldn't seem to get much further than burning the occasional CD. Her attempts at storing client photos were haphazard at best; her desk drawer was littered with un-

marked silver discs that found themselves sandwiched between paper clips and note cards. She had no idea how old the CDs were or what photographs were on them. She certainly didn't have time to check.

As she pressed back the metal tab on her diet cola can, her eyes darted between her CPU and her top drawer. The idea that her photos were such a critical part of her business and that she had no idea if they were protected made her cringe, but the idea of trying to create her own backup system was even more disheartening.

She'd put a few pictures on some CDs. That was better than nothing, right?

Tracy Laidlaw, president of Beyond Words, Ltd., is a woman with a background in technology with a lineage to match. Her father, Andy Marken, is the president of Marken Communications, a company that is extremely active in the photo industry. Tracy's pedigree and expertise still didn't protect her from losing three years of digital photographs as she worked on swapping out hard drives. In the process of upgrading her computer, she offloaded her files to a CD-RW, installed the new hard drive, and then accidentally wrote over all the data on the CD containing her photographs.

Andy jokes that Tracy is "old enough to know better," but he says it is a common issue with today's digital camera users — these files are in a far more tenuous state than most people realize. Fortunately, Tracy's assistant had tucked away the original hard drive, untying the knot in Tracy's stomach.

Many people aren't so lucky. Today's hard drives are bursting with digital photographs, but few of us pro-actively back up our files. In fact, IDC, a provider of market intelligence and analysis, estimates that only 15 percent of home users are actively backing up their hard drives, a statistic that Andy Marken finds frustrating. "This issue is even more critical now that people are happily shooting away with their digital cameras and dumping their images on their hard drives," he says, "because they think those images will be there forever. They won't."[5]

Snapshots

Did You Know?
Fuji built an empire in the Empire. In 1965, Fuji Photo Film U.S.A., Inc., was established in an office in the Empire State Building. The company started with only six employees.

A term often thrown around in the computing world is MTBF, which can mean (depending upon the application and context) either "mean time before failure" or "mean time between failures." Essentially, an MTBF number is an engineering estimate of how long a classification of hardware or electronic device will run under optimum conditions before experiencing a failure based on the combination of life expectancy for all of its components. While these numbers are estimates and the proper use and application of MTBF has been bantered about on many a blog and message board, the basic issue to remember is that while your experience *may* vary, these devices *will* fail at some point. That's what the MTBF is trying to indicate. In fact, most hard drives will fail during their MTBF period. Some devices last longer than others, but when it comes to your precious pictures, remember that your hard drive shouldn't be the *only* trustee of your images.

Stories about the damage to digital photographs have become more common as more and more people trade in their film cameras for digital models. Regardless of the format — online albums, CD-RW, DVD, camera card, or printed picture — one theme remains the same.

Loss.

No single solution is perfect, but if we can understand and respect each medium's weak spots, we can create a regular system designed to protect our images as they travel from our digital cameras to various storage devices, online, and beyond.

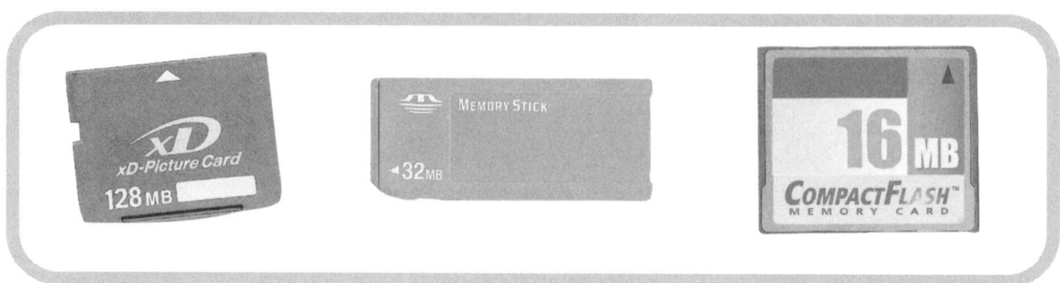

Photo 4A
The kind of media card you're using is determined by the camera you've chosen. Some models now come in sizes in the gigabyte range, making it highly unlikely you'll run out of room on your camera card during an event.

Digital Camera Cards

Digital camera memory cards are also called *media cards* or *removable media* and come in almost as many flavors as potato chips. Digital camera cards are getting larger than America's waistlines and cheaper than a clearance sale at the dollar store. The quality of digital cameras now rivals film, and today's models are priced to sell. Media cards were sometimes referred to as *digital film* to help people understand where the images resided in the camera, but they are now being marketed as a method of not only temporarily holding digital images until they reach the computer but as a way of permanently storing digital pictures.

Is this really a safe place to keep your photographs?

There are a number of different kinds of media cards — often referred to as *flash media* — to choose from. There are Compact Flash, SD media, Memory Stick (Sony's proprietary format), and others — and the digital camera you purchase primarily determines your selection of media card. There are a few camera models that handle multiple formats. Some formats, like the xD format that is less than one inch square, are so small that one needs to take extreme care not to lose the card. It's best to store those teeny cards in a carrying case or media wallet.

One of the challenges of storing all your photos on your digital media is that, in addition to price concerns, it is difficult to label those memory cards so that you know what is on each card. You simply can't whip out a pen and write "Vacation Photos 2006" on its surface. An important part of choosing how to best store your pictures is making sure that those images can be easily identified in the future. You'll want loved ones to discover those discs one day and be compelled to open the files because there are pictures of Grandma Mary on them.

In addition, the cheap price of a CD often makes it the best choice, especially for those with a large picture library. You may wish to save your removable media for capturing those images in your camera and using it as a temporary holding space only.

> **Snapshots**
>
> **On the Road**
>
> If you're going on a vacation, make sure that you have enough storage on your media card (download other pictures before venturing out) and verify that your camera battery is fully charged. Consider packing your battery charger, and if you're taking a laptop with you, don't forget your adapter card so that you can download pictures in case your card fills up.

Will It Fit?

The ability to instantly view our digital images sometimes encourages us to snap away without worrying about how many shots we've taken. Unlike a 35mm camera that clearly tells us that we've got five frames left on the roll, your media card may not give you a warning that you've only got room for three more pictures. (Some models offer countdowns, but you'll need to verify whether yours does.)

There are a few issues that affect how many pictures will fit on your card.

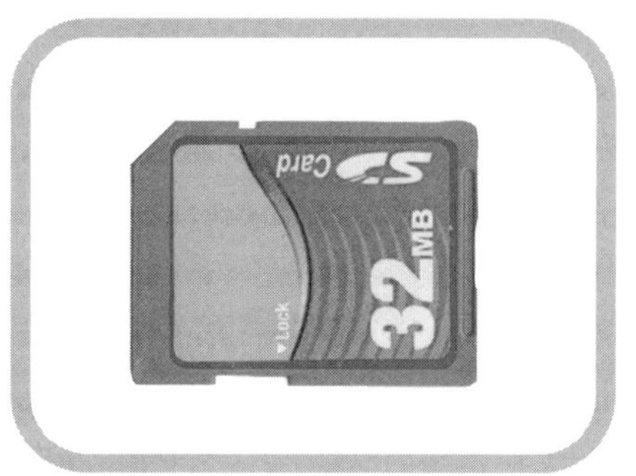

Photo 4B

Your digital camera probably came with a media card but you may find you quickly grow out of it. Today's digital media cards come in a variety of sizes, and today's prices allow you to get a lot of storage for just a little more money.

The first is the actual camera model. Digital camera models handle each file a bit differently, and you may find that there are slight variations in file size. The second issue is one of compression. Many of today's digital cameras allow you to choose to shoot your pictures in an uncompressed format, referred to as a *RAW file*, and these files take the most space on your camera card. You're likely familiar with the JPEG format (.jpg). These files have varying levels of compression. Shooting pictures in JPEG is extremely common because the file takes less space, still delivers a high-quality image, and is easily read by all current software programs.

However, JPEG compression uses a lossy compression method, which means it must discard a bit of the data in order to compress the file and make it take less space. When you open the file, the software has to interpolate, or re-constitute, the file by using mathematic algorithms. But this is not an exact science. The more a compressed file is opened, edited, and saved, the more deterioration your photos will experience over time. If you only do this a few times, the degradation is barely perceptible, and for most casual forms of photography, you may not notice it at all. It is not the opening, but the saving of the JPEG file, that can lead to image quality decreasing over time. Many of today's cameras have standard settings that balance providing a high-quality image with a specific compression ratio. If you'd like to learn more about how to change the compression settings on your camera, please refer to the manual.

For Advanced Users

For those who wish to maintain the highest quality images or wish to use advanced editing programs such as Adobe Photoshop, shooting RAW files may be the way to go. RAW files are popular with professional photographers who often have specialized applications and require the ability to greatly enlarge and enhance the images. There is a price for using this format; unlike JPEG or TIFF files, there is no standard for RAW files (although this is changing). The challenge is that those cameras capable of creating RAW files create their own unique, or proprietary, RAW file. This means that you may be unable to open your RAW files in your favorite image-editing program. Some cameras require you to use their specific software program to read the files, and there's no guarantee that this program will be available years from now, leaving your photographs in an unreadable format. The primary benefit of RAW files is that they are uncompressed and unprocessed by color algorithms, which means that you can control the color better in RAW files than in other formats. They also take up a great deal more space on your camera card. This issue is of particular interest to commercial or professional photographers (as well as some advanced amateurs or what we call *prosumers* in the industry).

Today's media cards are now available in one or two gigabyte models, giving today's shutterbug a license to shoot to her heart's content. You may want to rein that impulse in a bit, however, or at least make sure you quickly delete the poor shots, so that you won't have to wade through photos you really don't care about to find that perfect picture of your daughter with her prized sand castle.

(To figure out how many pictures you can fit on a camera card, check the quick reference guide in appendix A.)

Proper Care and Feeding of Digital Camera Cards

It's important to take great care when handling your digital media. There are a couple of major issues that can contribute to images becoming corrupted or lost. First of all, make sure to check your digital camera battery, because if it runs dry while operating, you run the risk of your current images — and your entire card — being corrupted. Worse yet, you may not realize the card is corrupted until you attempt to offload the images onto your computer. Second, make sure you never attempt to remove your digital camera media while the images are still transferring from the camera to the computer (or printer if you bypass this option). Digital cameras sometimes feed our impatience because they deliver so much so quickly, but resist the urge to tug until you can clearly see that the images are done transferring.

If you travel a little or a lot, you can rest assured knowing that your digital camera card should be fine when being x-rayed. A testing initiative led by the I3A (International Imaging Industry Association), SanDisk Corporation, and the U.S. Transportation Security Administration in 2004 concluded that the security scanner models in use do not damage today's digital camera cards. "Our tests should put travelers' fears to rest, that their digitally captured holiday memories won't be damaged in transit," says Lisa Walker, I3A president. "Digital cameras and media can safely go in carryons without the need for hand-inspection, which will simplify security checks and make those long lines move a little faster."[6]

Computer Hard Drives

If you're like most of today's digital camera users, you're using your family computer as the central holding facility for your library of digital cam-

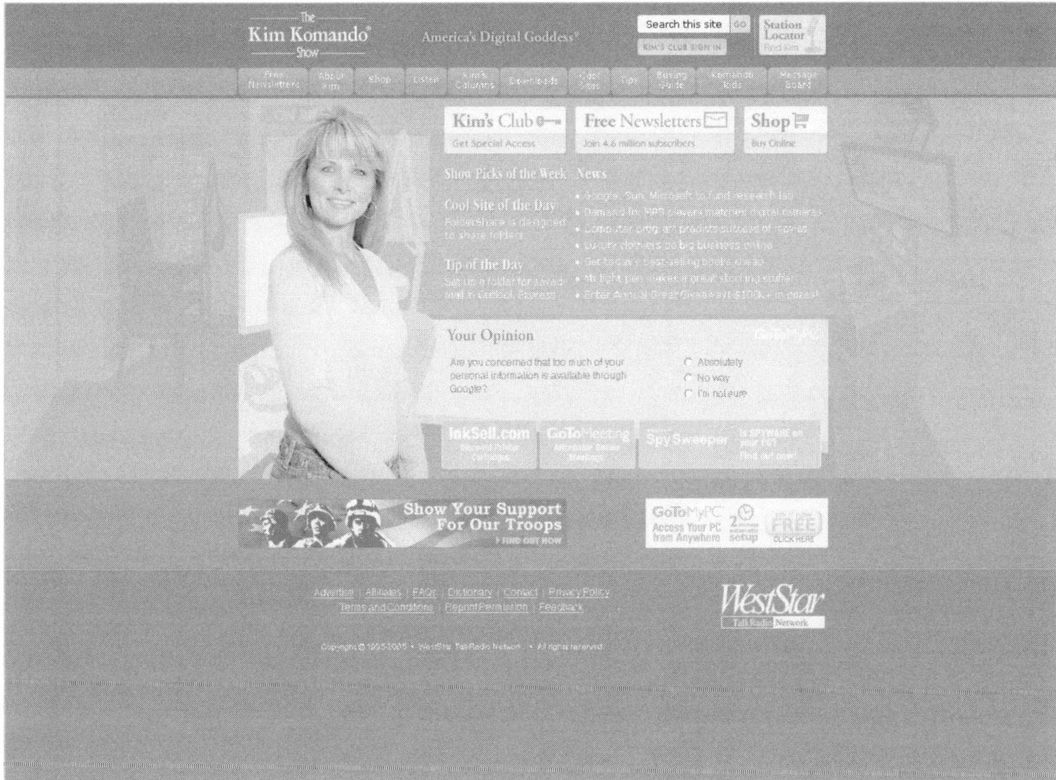

Photo 4D

You'll find a wealth of information on sites such as these to help you better understand the specifics of digital photography and how to best archive your digital pictures. *Image reproduced with permission from Kim Komando.*

era pictures. Maybe you're putting all your images in a general My Pictures folder and feeling some comfort that at least those images are all together, but if your photos still have those uninventive (and a bit maddening) general file names such as DSC_00214.jpg, we want to help you create a better method for managing and storing those images.

First, there are several great software programs available today that will help you easily manage your digital photographs (See chapter 3 for more information).And remember, if you aren't using any image management software, make sure your subfolders are set up under the My Pictures icon on your computer. It's best to prepare these subfolders ahead of time. This will relieve some pressure each time you go to offload your images, knowing that they're to be put in a specifically designated place.

Snapshots

For the Kids — Be Candid

Some of my absolute favorite photographs are ones of my children taken through a window as they play together outside. They may not even be aware of the camera, and in these instances, I'm able to capture their absolute essence.

Hard Drive or Heartbreak?

Backing up our computer hard drives ranks right up there with getting an annual physical; we know it's important, but we often put it off when other pressures encroach upon our time. Stephen Covey, the internationally acclaimed best-selling author of *The Seven Habits of Highly Effective People*, speaks of the differences between important and urgent tasks. Urgent tasks, like a pressing deadline or a ringing telephone, often take priority over important tasks such as getting exercise, playing outdoors with our kids, and yes, properly caring for our most precious photographs. Action is often taken only after our hard drive begins to make a sound similar to a coffee grinder, rewarding our carelessness with cryptic computer commands. It is at that point that we realize just how much we have lost.

Take heart! Protecting your photographs is easier than you may think, but it does require action. First and foremost, make sure that your computer is protected by anti-virus software and a firewall. Kim Komando, a nationally-syndicated talk show host and self-proclaimed "digital goddess," offers a number of recommendations regarding anti-virus software and firewall programs on her website at www.komando.com. The benefit of

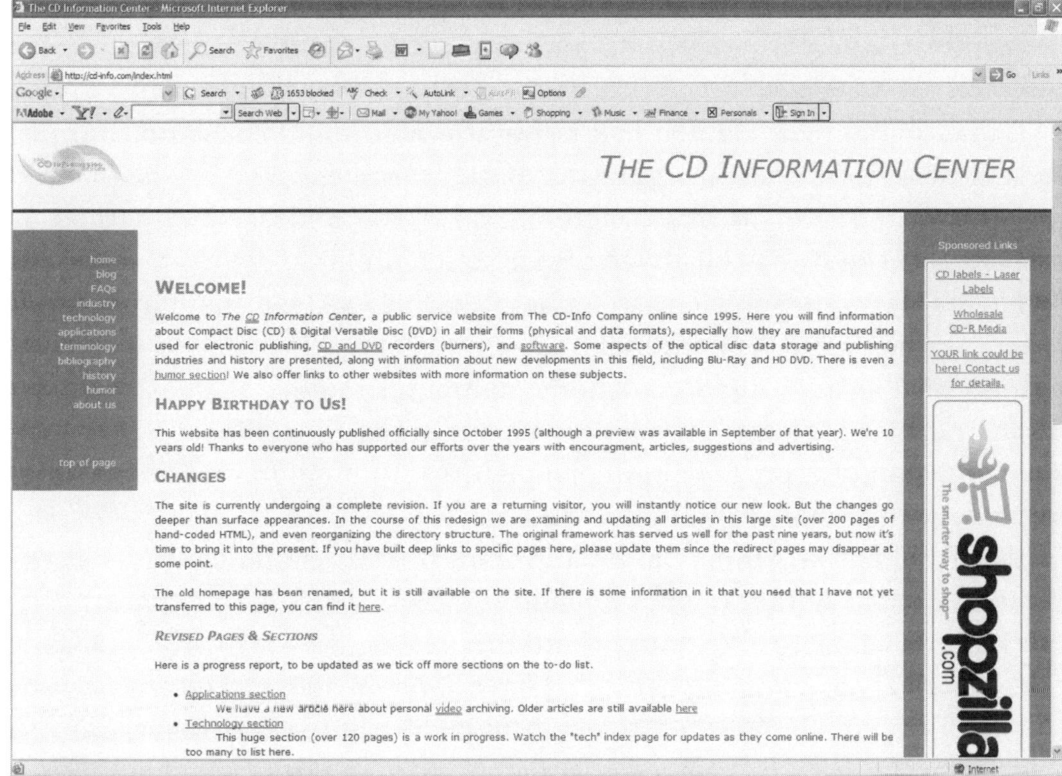

Photo 4E

You'll find a wealth of information on sites such as these to help you better understand the specifics of digital photography and how to best archive your digital pictures. *Image reproduced with permission from Katherine Cochrane.*

using a site such as hers is that you know these programs are properly tested and come from reliable sources. Also, many of these programs offer trial or demo versions for free. This is an important first step in protecting your digital pictures.

Another resource for information comes from Katherine Cochrane, founder and president of the CD-Info Company. Her website has a host of great information and is extremely valuable to those wanting to better understand the many aspects of CD and DVD media and the historical evolution of these formats. You can access her site at www.cd-info.com.

It may sound redundant, and it is, but it's important to back up your images in two places. Most people back up their images on CD media (a topic that is covered later in this chapter), and if you choose this method of archiving, make sure to burn two copies. Some prefer to diversify and store some images online with a trusted photo-sharing site (see chapter 5 on this topic). It's best to make sure that one set of backups is located in a different physical location than your home computer in case of catastrophe or some unexpected event. The cliché of not keeping all your eggs in one basket can certainly apply to your digital pictures. Your CDs may survive water, but they won't make it through a fire.

In our home, we employ a few different processes and continue to experiment as our library of digital pictures grows. In addition to backing up our hard drive using an external hard drive designed to "mirror" the content, we also back up using DVDs, and have some images stored with an online service. We also use a P2P (peer-to-peer) photo-sharing program (a topic covered later in the book), which allows us to send photographs directly to loved ones (rather than attaching them to an email) so that additional high-resolution copies available in other locations. I tend to only send my favorites, so if I ever needed copies, I could always call my mom or mother-in-law.

Many experts state that how often you back up depends upon how important the information is and how often it changes. Every time you upload important photographs, add a few minutes to back them up. Some programs now include backup functions to make this process easier. If you're unable to do both downloading and backing up during one sitting, consider backing up on a regular basis, such as monthly or seasonally. Just make sure you do it!

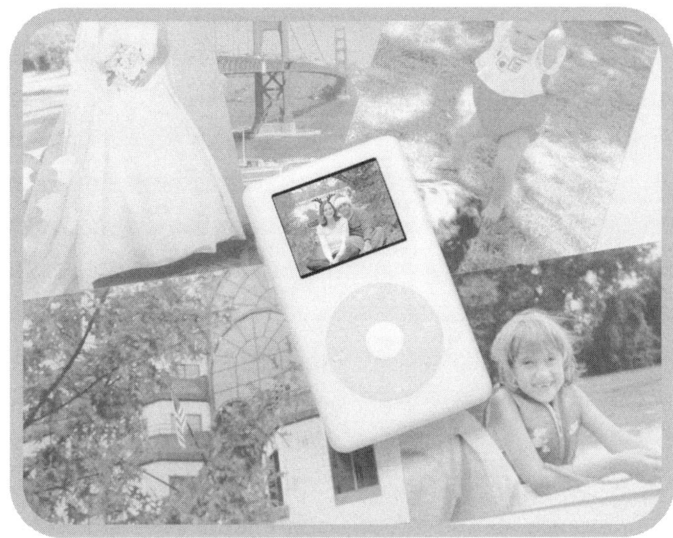

Photo 4E
The Apple iPod is a great way to enjoy your favorite photographs while keeping them safe (and portable) in case a hard drive crash occurs. *Photograph & design courtesy of John McDavitt.*

Photo Vaults, Photo Wallets, and Other Nifty Items

A slew of new terms such as *photo vaults*, *photo wallets*, and *mobile media hard drives* all describe a new generation of hardware designed to help today's digital camera users offload their digital pictures from their media cards onto a more permanent storage device. Apple's iPod line, which includes several models that can hold photographs and videos in addition to music and podcasts, can be another great way to enjoy your digital pictures while backing them up in another location.

For Advanced Users

Dedicated photo vaults are essentially small mobile hard drives that easily connect to your camera through a USB port, allowing you to offload your pictures from the memory card. These units have a respectable CD screen for viewing, which also comes in handy to help you delete the less-than-stellar shots. These vaults are also designed to connect to your tele-

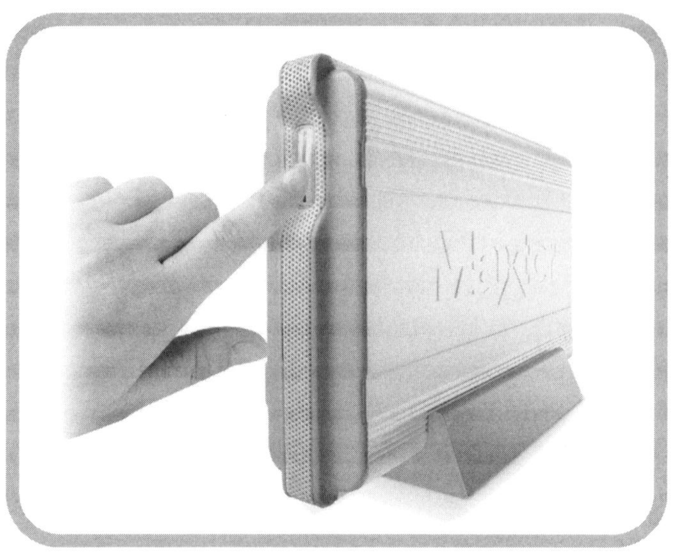

Photo 4F
External drives, such as the Maxtor OneTouch II, make backing up your hard drive far less cumbersome than in years past. Reproduced with permission from Maxtor.

vision so that you can view your photos in style. Another benefit of these devices is that they have their own memory card slots and their own battery. Digital camera batteries are often quickly drained by their own LCD screens, and many photo vaults don't require the camera to provide power.

These units aren't nearly as slim and sleek as an iPod, but they are geared more toward sharing and storage than mobile entertainment. Still, if you're looking for a more comprehensive way of storing your pictures and doing so in a way that gives you the ability to view, select, and share on other entertainment devices (such as television), this can be a solid selection in your image preservation toolkit.

For those looking for a simple solution to simply offload digital pictures and keep them protected, a removable USB flash drive is a popular choice. These slim units are shorter than a standard pen, have some password protection features to access files, and plug directly into the USB port of your computer. They operate as a drive, much like your CD writer. These units are simple, fast, and portable, and many traveling executives use them to transport important files. Sensitive company information, personal information, and precious photos are lost as the incidence of laptop theft continues to grow. Having these files on a removable USB flash drive is a way to ensure your pictures are backed up and better shielded from hard drive failure or theft.

Snapshots

Did You Know?
Polaroid photography was invented by Edwin Land. His single-step process for processing and printing photographs was truly considered a photographic revolution. He founded his company, Polaroid, and the first camera was sold to consumers in 1948.

CD-R, CD-RW, or DVD: Which Is Best for Photos?

If you're already using a method of backing up your photos, you've likely chosen the CD format to accomplish this task. Blank CDs are often cheaper than a burrito at Taco Bell and can be found in almost every retail store from supermarkets to office supply shops, consumer electronics stores to warehouse supply stores. While it may seem that all CDs are created equal, this is simply not the case. Our impulse may be to buy the cheapest media, but we're talking about protecting your digital pictures here, so we need to take a bit more care.

For those of you interested in the next generation technologies of HD-DVD and Blu-ray (think VHS vs. Beta), please see chapter 9, "Ahead of the Curve — Keeping up with Changing Technology." This issue will eventually affect you as one of these will be the future DVD format, and neither of them is designed to be compatible with the current DVD players found in homes across the country. That said, while you may need a new player, experts indicate that existing DVDs will still be able to be read and recorded. Your pictures will still be accessible, but you will likely have to invest in a new DVD player in the future.

To CD-R or to CD-RW: That Is the Question

Should you put your photos on a CD-R, a CD-RW, or a DVD? For photographs, you can rely on any one of these choices, but you may wish to consider a few things before making your final decision. The first choice is the CD, and we will group the CD-R and the CD-RW categories together. A standard CD holds 700 MB of information, which will translate into approximately several hundred high-quality color photographs. The CD format has been in existence for almost 25 years and has continued to evolve and improve. It's also a format that is ubiquitous in that most of the BILLION computers that have been sold to date have a CD player built into them. This means that you can send a CD to almost anyone you know with a computer, and they'll be equipped to read the files (and view the pictures).

So, if you want to use CDs, which is the best method — CD-R or CD-RW? Some people gravitate toward CD-RW, or rewritable CDs, because well, they're rewritable, and you can go back to add more information. This is true, but it can also mean that you accidentally erase your pictures. Andy Marken cautions, "When it comes to pictures, I recommend using the CD-R format because, while you may not be able to add to the CD later, you won't be able to write over the existing data, either. The concept of editing and reusing the media is valid. However, most people quickly find that they do not delete or overwrite photo data because they 'just know' that the moment a photo is deleted or erased… that will be just the photo they must have and it is gone. So to be safe they use a new disc. We advise people to err on the side of caution."[7] Regardless of which format you choose, it's important to treat your CDs with great care, much like you would handle a roll of film. Creating a simple strategy and taking a few minutes to devise a process will mean a great deal of time and frustration is saved the next time you need to get your hands on that birthday party photo for your scrapbook project.

Here are a few tips when managing and storing your CDs:

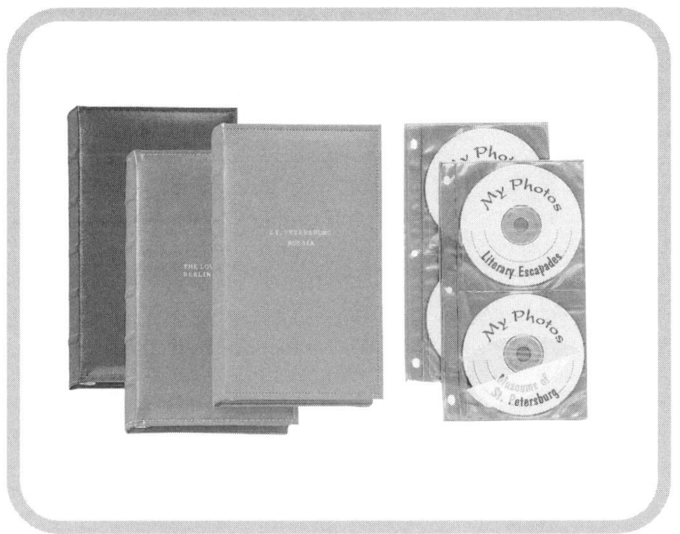

Photo 4G
You can find many products, such as this line of albums from Exposures, designed specifically for storing both your hard copy pictures and your digital files. *Reproduced with permission from Exposures — www.exposuresonline.com*

- Use CD-R rather than the CD-RW format to insure you don't overwrite your images. The prices are so low that they make the best choice. If you're worried about keeping up with changing technology, consider storing your pictures on DVD (the prices are extremely low now but these discs must be handled with extreme care) and copy your CD-R files to a new DVD. (See next section on DVD.)

- Consider grouping your photos by key event, year, or in a grouping method that makes sense to you.

- Handle your CDs by the center hole or the outer edge, and take care not to scratch the bottom.

- If writing on the CD surface (e.g., Vacation 2006), make sure to use a non-permanent marker, as permanent markers have powerful solvents that can eat through a label over time and damage the disc.

- Store your CDs upright (in a book style) and in jewel cases or specialty albums to protect them. Keep them in a cool, dry place.

- Make a duplicate set and keep them in another location in case of a catastrophe (yes, this does happen!).

- Check your CDs on a regular basis (I recommend every year) to make sure the files open and that the pictures can be accessed (yes, this happens too!).

The CD format does have the benefit of history on its side. Because they've been part of our computing existence for the last two decades, they can be counted on to be available and readable for some time. Marken calls CD media "the floppy disk of the twenty-first century,"[8] because they are so widely available and inexpensive. Does that mean, however, that they're in jeopardy of being obsolete like the floppy in twenty to thirty years? Should you move to DVD instead?

DVD Digital Photo Albums

Some people choose DVD media, which has become more cost effective than ever before. DVD's appeal is due largely to the fact that, in addition to being seen as more contemporary than the standard CD, a single-layer DVD is capable of holding 4.7 gigabytes, which translates into thousands of high-quality photographs. Even those families that snap away with reckless abandon would be able to keep years of pictures on a single DVD. Of course, it wouldn't be prudent to wait three or four years to burn a DVD in order to take full advantage of its capacity, and since DVDs cost more than CDs, price is another issue to take into account.

IDC estimates that there are over 120 million DVD recorders or drives in existence worldwide, and more than half of the homes that have DVD players have two or more. With experts forecasting that about 80 percent of all U.S. households will have a DVD player by the end of 2005, this format is demonstrating the same vast adoption as its CD predecessor. It seems that the DVD is the hands-down choice. For many, the DVD is the clear choice due to its technology, its ability to hold countless albums, and its efficacy. It also is attractive because this format is considered more current and is likely to have a longer life than the CD, which some fear will go the way of the floppy disk. Also, continued price drops make this format a top choice for protecting your images into the future.

However, some experts caution against using DVDs for long-term storage of digital pictures unless you intend to take great care with how they are handled. Katherine Cochrane of CD-Info comments that DVDs are a much more dense media than CDs. A fingerprint or a smudge on a DVD could greatly impact the tightly packed data.

Single-Layer or Double-Layer DVD?

A single-layer DVD holds 4.7 gigabytes of information vs. the 8.5 held by a double-layer DVD. While the price for double-layer DVDs are still much higher than the single-layer version, several industry experts believe this will change, making the double-layer version a better choice in the future. You can't really go wrong in this arena as long as you pick quality media,back up on a regular basis, and treat your DVDs with great care. The current life expectancy of a DVD (using quality media) is approximately one hundred years. The key will be to make sure your archives are transferred to a new format when DVD is replaced a few decades down the road.

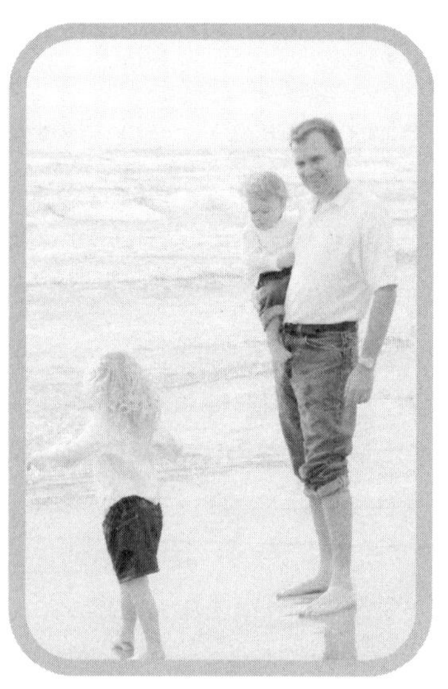

Photo 4H
Printing your pictures is more than just a way to rescue memories trapped on your computer; they are also a great back up method to protect those precious moments in case catastrophe strikes.

In fact, some industry experts note that the archival issue of CDs and DVDs isn't as important when evaluating a 60- vs. a 100-year life span as the issue of making sure your pictures aren't trapped on a media format that can no longer be read is. For those of you who have a desk drawer full of floppy disks, the issue is essentially the same. The disks may still be readable, but they can't be read. Note the lack of a floppy drive in today's breed of computers and laptops.

The Printed Picture: Another Important Backup Strategy

With so much emphasis on pictures as digital files, it makes sense that we would look to other electronic formats when creating a backup strategy, but many find the printed picture is the perfect backup solution. Statistics show that even though we're taking more pictures than ever, the rate at which we're printing is declining. This is due, in part, to the fact that we are now getting instant gratification by viewing our images on our LCD screens and computers rather than waiting at the photo lab for prints.

Mitch Goldstone, the owner of 30 Minute Photos Etc., in Irvine, California, is an avid spokesman for the photo industry and supports many local causes through his business. He also knows what it feels like to lose precious photographs. He lost all of his digital photographs a few years ago when his laptop hard drive crashed. "Fortunately, I own a photo business and I had prints,"[9] he said in a recent interview with *Picture Business* magazine.

The printed picture offers many tangible benefits. It can be easily retrieved and favorite pictures can be readily identified – you just need to look at them to decide which ones matter most. Many digital papers last a lifetime (see chapter 6 on digital prints) and will stand the test of time, especially when they are handled and stored properly. Also, printed pictures can be scanned in an emergency to recreate a digital photo archive. The quality may vary due to the paper the picture was printed on and the kind of scanner being used (matte finish generally doesn't scan quite as well as glossy because the scanner picks up the pebbled surface), but at least a hard copy can be replicated. If a digital file is corrupted, sometimes it can be restored, but sometimes it's lost for good.

Some experts recommend that once a year, favorite photographs should be printed either at a trusted retail store that uses archival papers (those that have digital minilabs that print on silver-halide paper) or by using a trusted online service that promotes using archival materials. If the digital files should ever be corrupted or destroyed, at least you'll have a hard copy in hand.

So, when in doubt, print it out.

The Big Picture

When it comes to your computer's hard drive, it's best to spread the risk. Most people simply don't realize the statistical risk of keeping their pictures exclusively on their hard drive. Let it continue serving as the central storage device for your images but don't rely on it as a permanent archive. Burning a DVD and printing your pictures may take a bit of time, but the effort will be repaid many times over. You'll experience some relief knowing your pictures are protected, and you'll enjoy another stroll down memory lane in the process.

- Only 15 percent of home computer users currently back up their computers, yet more than half of consumers will experience data and picture loss through a hard drive crash.

- To manage and locate your digital pictures, try one of the many low-priced or free software programs available. Some programs create automatic albums based upon the metadata on the files, quickly creating a chronological album for you to review. Many of these programs also include CD and DVD backup functions.

- When considering a backup strategy, make sure your plan includes two distinct places for digital pictures with one set of backups stored someplace other than in your home.

- When backing up images to CD or DVD, consider which format would work best and make sure to handle them with the same care as you would handle film.

- Pick a time frame each year (or season) to back up your pictures and also to check past backups to ensure the files can still be opened and accessed.

- A recent study states that your camera cards will be fine going through the standard x-ray machines if you're traveling.

- When a new archive format comes out, migrate your archive but keep the older discs as additional insurance.

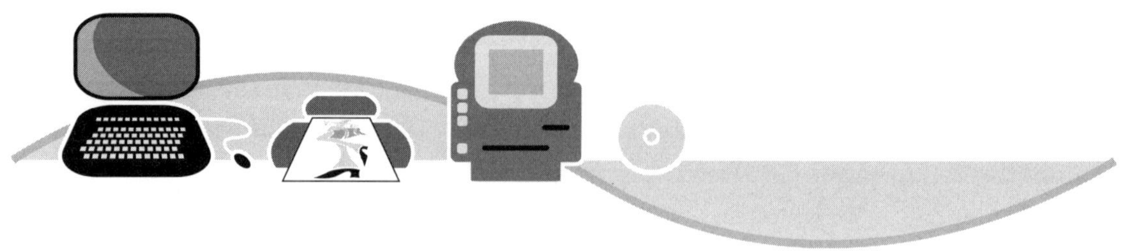

5

Photography on the Web

Email, Online Albums, and More

Natalie sighed in exasperation as she walked by her dining room, which had served as a storage space since her family's move months before. Nagging worries around verifying she was finally receiving all the right mail and attending to the countless loose ends that accompany a move across the country plagued her on a regular basis. Would she ever feel as though she had finally settled in? One thing she hadn't done was add more pictures to her online photo album. In fact, she couldn't remember the last time she'd logged into the account at all. "I must have over a hundred pictures to upload," she said to herself as she visualized her to-do list unfolding on an endless ream of paper like a scroll from the Middle Ages. At least she knew where the pictures were and could just add to the album.

"No time like the present," she said and sat down at her computer. Her first attempt to log in yielded an "invalid log in" message. "Oh, that's right," she remembered, "this must still have my old email address listed." She tried another email address — the one she'd abandoned last year after receiving too much SPAM *— and found it, too, wasn't recognized. Proving to herself that the definition of insanity is to do the same thing over and over and expect different results, she typed in the same two email addresses and was rewarded with the same response: "invalid log in." After muttering language not fit for her children to hear, she powered off her system and headed for bed.*

Natalie made an effort to get to work extra early the next morning to allow her time to call the online company for help. She began worrying about the fact that she couldn't access her online albums. Her intuition proved correct.

"I'm sorry, ma'am," the service representative replied. "Your account was deleted last month."

"What?" Natalie said with an angry voice that echoed off her office walls. "How on Earth could you just delete all those pictures?"

The representative remained polite and calmly explained, "I see here that we sent several email notifications to you that your pictures would be deleted if you didn't order anything from the site. We state this policy plainly in our Terms of Agreement. We would have mailed you a postcard, too, but you didn't list your mailing address in your contact information."

Disheartened, she offered a barely audible thanks and hung up the phone. She couldn't believe the company would delete her pictures, but she also couldn't believe that she didn't understand the terms. As a lawyer, she knew better. Ignorance of a policy is no excuse. She often wondered how companies could offer unlimited storage online and now she knew. These were businesses that needed to sell products, and the agreement to purchase something — even one 4 x 6 print — was required to continue storing photographs on the company's server. They had tried to contact her, but she had abandoned the email address and never updated her account.

Remembering that some of those photos were scattered between her computer and her husband's laptop, she thought of the effort that lie ahead.

"Live and learn," she sighed to herself as she went to retrieve another cup of coffee. "Live and learn."

While this particular story is fiction, the issue is quite real. I am a big fan of online photo sites and use a couple of them regularly. They are a fantastic way to get quality digital prints, to share pictures with loved ones, and manage your library of photographs. Regardless of what you may perceive, many of these services are not available on an unlimited basis for an unlimited period of time without some purchase from you. Several newspapers and magazines have covered specific incidents where people have lost their entire digital photo albums because the company deleted them. Most of these companies don't do this lightly — they will make several attempts to contact you and let you know of this impending event — but it is up to you to be aware of the company's terms and to make sure your account information is kept current. There are some companies that do not have a deletion policy, meaning they will keep your pictures indefinitely, but it is important to ask this question so you understand the terms of agreement.

The critical issue to remember is that *you* are ultimately responsible for the proper care and storage of your digital pictures. Online processing services have only been in existence for about seven or eight years. They are in a stage of growing up, much like digital photography itself, so the onus is on the picture taker to understand the risks and rewards and to use online services in a way that best utilizes their strengths. These sites are business entities and need to have paying customers as clients.

Warnings aside, I highly recommend that you consider an online service as part of your backup strategy. Having your photos stored in another location by a professional company with a solid reputation is a great way to make sure you have access to your pictures (as well as a method of ordering digital prints, photo books, and other items). Many of these companies also now offer archival CDs, so that you can receive a backup of the images you've uploaded to the site. Consider taking advantage of this service, as it will save you time and will provide another layer of safety in protecting your photographs.

The Internet has proven itself to be a fantastic partner for digital photography; in fact, online photo albums have become so popular that many use them as the primary method of sharing and storing their photographs. After all, some of these companies are owned by large film-based behemoths or other longstanding institutions, so it seems that the criteria of using a brand name you trust is all you really need to consider (in addition to the pricing structure). And many of us do just that.

This may work for some people and not others. Spend a few minutes on different sites to decide which have the tools, overall feel, or navigation that fits your style. Can you easily upload pictures and create different albums? Can you find what you're looking for without going on an exhaustive search of mouse clicks? Are there other services you find interesting that you might purchase now or in the near future?

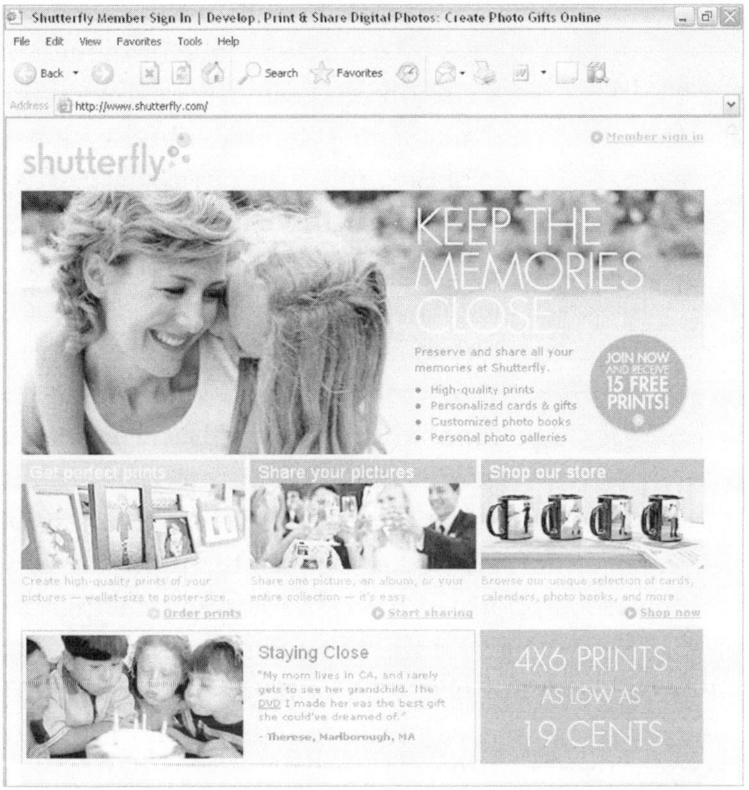

Photo 5A

Some photo sites, like Shutterfly.com, don't have a deletion policy and offer a variety of digital photo services. Photograph courtesy of Shutterfly.

It is also possible to combine the benefits of the Internet with the expertise and convenience of your favorite local store. Many local retailers offer online services whereby you can order your prints from home and pick them up an hour later in the store. This is a great option for those who want to spend a bit of time enhancing and sorting their photos from home and then simply pick up the print order the next time they're out running errands. It can also save you some money in postage.

Snapshots

For the Best Kid Photos

Be realistic, especially when you have more than one kid. They may not all be smiling at the same time or all looking at the camera. If the smiles are genuine and they look like they're having fun, that's the best possible picture.

Online photo processing and storage companies invest a great deal of money in their infrastructure and the cost of storing images online. Considering that each high-quality photograph is between two and five megabytes in size, it actually adds up to *a lot* of money. They simply can't afford to offer free storage forever without any commitment on our part to purchase prints or other products.

That said, the section of a service agreement that few people read is not the place to communicate that important information, and some companies are working to better articulate this issue to customers. In today's global economy, many people regularly move for career opportunities or for family obligations. With so much involved in simply relocating, few people think to update their contact information for their online photo storage service. After all, you know where the photos are located. Isn't that enough?

Storing Your Photos Online

There is now a new breed of online photo company designed specifically to protect and store digital photographs. These are different from the online services for sharing photos and printing photos.

It's important for you to know what you really want. Do you want an online service for sharing photos, printing photos, protecting photos, or a combination of all three? Some companies provide long-term backup services for corporations and are now extending their services to individuals. These companies provide secure online storage and access for a monthly fee (see more in the resources section of this book). Once you have a better understanding of how you intend to use your photos, you'll be able to

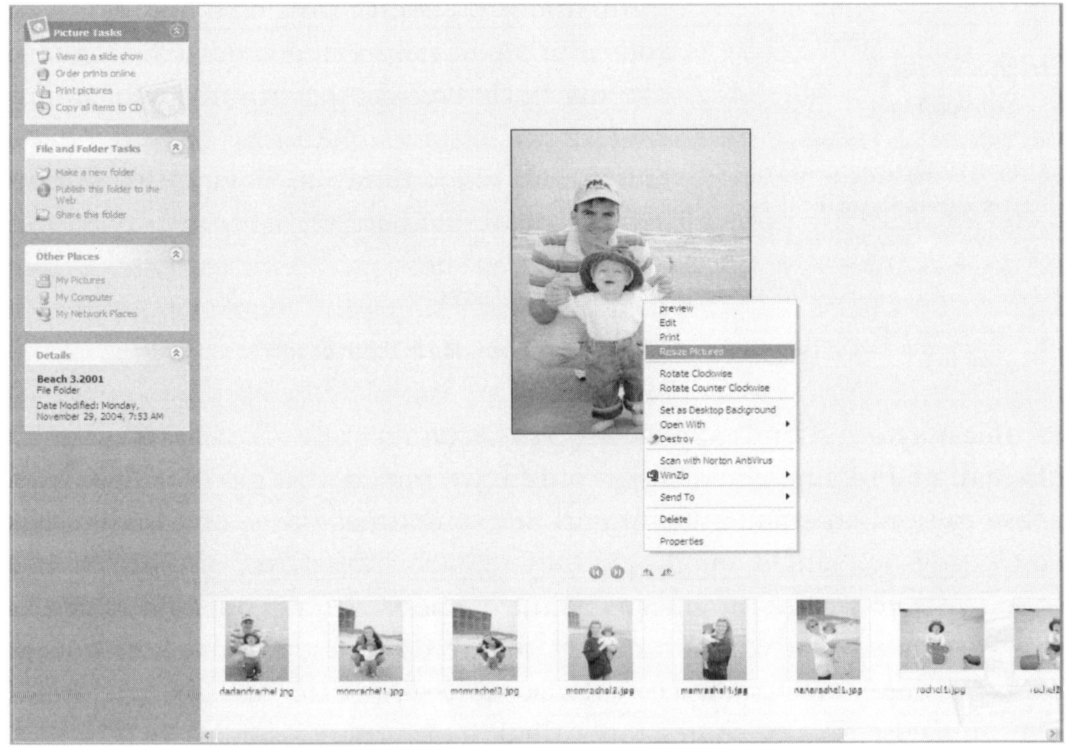

Photo 5B

Consider using some free tools, like Microsoft's Image Resizer, which helps you resize pictures with a mouse click so that you're sending the right size for the web or to be used as an email attachment. *Microsoft product screen shot(s) reprinted with permission from Microsoft Corporation.*

narrow down the choices and find a service that will meet your needs, saving you the agony of possibly losing your photos or trying to relocate them to another service at a later date.

Some companies now promote online file storage for those needing to share, back up, and store large amounts of data such as photos, music, software, and other items. You can find these companies through a simple online search using keywords such as *storing photos online* or *back up files online.* Several companies extend these services to both home users and

Snapshots

Did You Know?
Kodak's Dollar Store — Kodak's Brownie camera was introduced to the public in 1900 and sold for just one dollar.

companies and even provide simple software and tutorials to help you get started. If you're like my husband, who has spent a substantial amount of time organizing photographs, music, and video libraries, having this option to back up all that hard work is one way to protect all that effort.

Attaching Photos to Your Email

Many of us are inundated with photo email attachments from friends and family. It's certainly one of the easiest ways to share digital pictures, and if you only have one or two pictures, it makes sense to send an email attachment. But sometimes I'll receive a dozen or so pictures in a single email, and they're each a megabyte or more. If you want to simply share the images, you can choose from a host of image-editing programs that will automatically size down the pictures for you to send via email. Windows XP will also help you automatically size down your images with a great free tool called the Image Resizer. It can be found in Microsoft's PowerToys section on the company's website, and it allows you to resize your images with a right click of your mouse. And the price is right. It's free. Resizing photos for email use or to be used on eBay has never been easier.

If you think the recipient wants a high-resolution file because it's your mother and she wants to print the picture at home or take the file to her local drugstore to be printed, then attaching the picture is fine. Just remember that some people are still saddled with a dial-up connection (including my own mother), so don't send a bunch of files that will clog up the receiver's email box. If you prefer to send an email attachment rather than use an online site, just make sure to do the following:

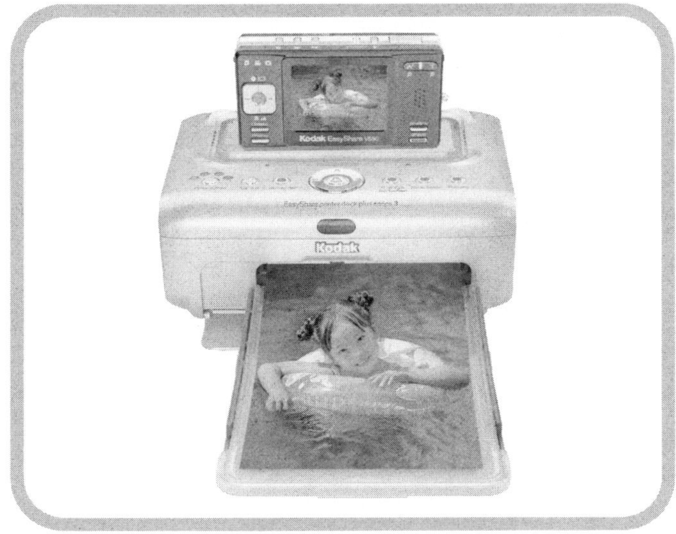

Photo 5C
Some digital cameras, such as the Kodak EasyShare v550 and printer dock, allow you to bypass your computer entirely to print high quality digital photographs. *Image reproduced with permission from Eastman Kodak Company.*

- **Send few and far between.** People love the occasional "isn't she adorable" shot but quickly tire of a weekly barrage of multiple email pictures. Pick your favorite and send it, and remember to let some time pass before sending another one (unless your mom says she really wants to see all twenty shots of your child's first attempt at using a spoon!).

- **Size it down.** If the purpose is only to share the image (not to print it), make sure to send a lower resolution file. (This is addressed in detail later in this chapter.)

- **Query your address book.** Simply asking your friends and loved ones if they'd like to receive pictures from time to time means a great deal to the recipients. They will appreciate your consideration and may be more receptive to photos in the future. Plus, you can identify those

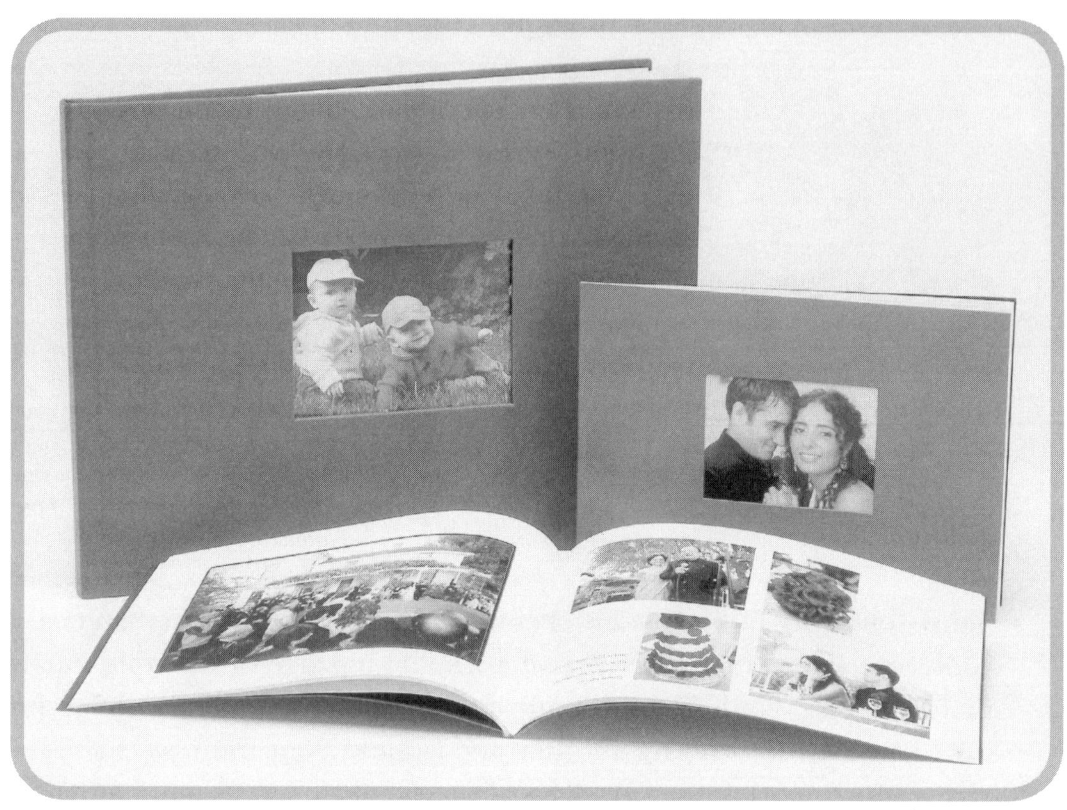

Photo 5D

Photo books are quickly becoming one of the most popular items offered by online photo services. For those who are intimidated by traditional scrapbooking but wish to tell a story through photography, these photo books are a great alternative. *Photo courtesy of Shutterfly.*

who really relish those regular emails and you can make sure to indulge them!

Camera Docking Station

For those who are anxious to get digital pictures in hand soon after the pictures have been taken, using a digital camera with a compatible docking station is one way of rescuing your photographs from your computer and bringing them center stage in frames or on your refrigerator door.

If you have a docking station for your camera, you can set up an email address list for it, and this process is pretty simple. Just make sure to integrate those photos into your master image library on your computer so that they're included in your archives and in your backups. Today's media cards are in the gigabyte and higher range, so it may be tempting to let your images pile up on the camera card since the initial excitement of emailing your photos has passed. Resist this urge by setting up some sort of regular schedule to keep images from getting lost, overwritten, or lost in transition.

Online Photo Albums

There are several excellent online photo companies capable of helping you manage, share, and print your digital pictures. You'll want to make sure that you take advantage of the many tools they offer while not getting bogged down with features or other things that are of little interest to you. If you'd like to use an online album for the long-term sharing, storing, and printing of your pictures or as a backup strategy for your hard-drive, consider taking the following actions:

- Only upload your favorite pictures.
- Create albums with a naming scheme (vacation, year, event, and so on) so you'll be able to locate them later.
- If the site allows you to add text or words for searching features, use this feature but keep it simple. Use a range of a few words (all lowercase) and use that list consistently so pictures don't fall off your radar.

- If you use the photos for business or clients, create separate directories or accounts for those clients.

- Keep your account information current and use your home information as opposed to your business address to make sure you receive updates from your online service provider.

Just because online photo sites state you can upload freely doesn't mean you should. Use a site with care and as a resource so that you can easily locate, share, and print the pictures that matter the most to you. Not only will it help you keep your friends from being bored when looking at the photos, it will also help you better manage your burgeoning digital library. A little restraint now can translate into a great deal of satisfaction for years to come.

I must admit that I marvel at some of the scrapbooks I've seen. The amount of creativity and time it takes to create such beautiful keepsakes is not an effort to be taken lightly. Scrapbooking has become an increasingly important segment of the imaging industry, because digital photography has made creating these works of art easier and more convenient than ever before. The number of "croppers," as they are often called, are growing in record numbers.

However, if you're like me (who has been known to wield a glue gun only to find it stuck to the carpet moments later), you may want to try your hand at online scrapbooking. There are several companies that offer wonderful scrapbooking or "photo book" products, and these options are a great way to dip your toe into the scrapbook arena.

Once you upload your pictures, you'll find several templates that you can move around like puzzle pieces to fill each page. Many have sections for journaling so that you can provide the proper backstory about why each image is special or what was going on in your lives during that time period. You may find that the combination of the pictures and the back story pro-

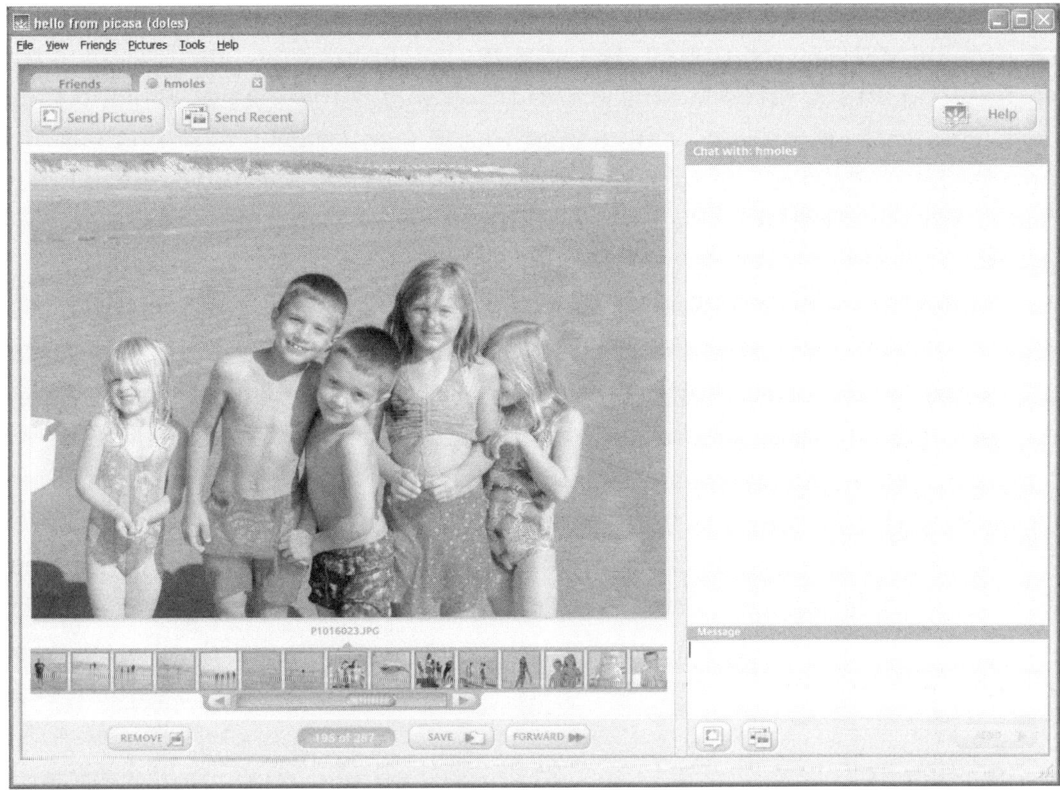

Photo 5E
Programs such as Google's Hello are similar to instant messaging programs but allow you to share photos in addition to online conversation. *Reprint permission granted by Google.*

vide a better understanding of the images you've chosen to include. This method can also ensure that others in the photographs (aunts, uncles, cousins, and close friends) are properly named so that your children aren't pointing to a picture asking, "Who's that guy, Mom?"

Peer-to-Peer Photo Sharing

There is a new breed of software application popping up in cyberspace.

Peer-to-peer photo sharing applications (P2P) are essentially programs that let you directly share digital pictures with friends and family. P2P programs are a bit like instant messenger programs, allowing you to send files back and forth to other people using the same software and even chat online at the same time. Some even integrate with image-editing programs, making it easier than ever to keep photos from loved ones in a central image library.

Some of the most popular programs include Google's Hello, ShareALot, and PiXPO. These programs each have their own strengths and weaknesses, but you'll quickly find one that you enjoy using. Some of these programs allow you to send a high-resolution file so that loved ones can print the pictures if they choose and also offer file encryption so that no one else can access the pictures on your hard drive.

For a listing of P2P programs and other information, check the "Resources" section.

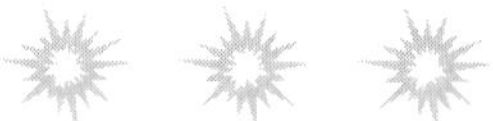

If you give thought to how you intend to retrieve, use, store, and print your digital pictures once they've been uploaded, you'll find a solution far better tailored to your needs than simply responding to the latest marketing ploy touting super cheap digital prints or unlimited storage. These offers always come with a price. Just make sure you know what it is.

The Big Picture

If you haven't tried an online service yet, now is the time to jump in. Not only will it serve as an important part of your backup strategy, it is a great way to stay connected with loved ones and help you turn your pictures into family chronicles. Photo books and other products offered online (which are also available in some retail stores) are a fantastic way to turn your photographs into lifetime stories.

- Determine how you want to use your online photo service. Will you only be sharing through email and albums or do you want the ability to print and create other products or novelties?
- Remember that many online storage companies do not provide long-term storage without a purchase. If you don't understand the terms, the company may have the right to delete your digital pictures within a certain time frame.
- Always keep your profile (contact) information current and accurate. If there is an issue with your account or your files, you'll want to make sure the notifications reach you so that you can respond.
- Make sure to filter your photos before uploading them so that you've only uploaded the images you really care about. Don't upload all of your images or you'll have a hard time filtering and moving them later.

- Remember that if you want to send an email file as an attachment (directly to someone else), don't send the high-resolution file. If you're going to upload it to an online processing/printing site, send the high-resolution file so that you are able to print a quality photograph.

- When using a "docking" digital camera that doesn't require a PC, don't forget to integrate those images into your master computer library so that they're included in your files and in your regular archiving schedule.

- Remember that using an online storage site is a great way to back up your images and protect them from a hard drive crash or memory card failure.

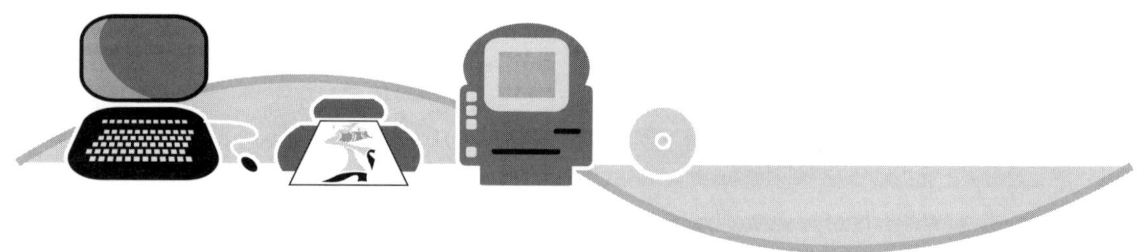

6

Picture Perfect

Making Sure Your Printed Pictures Last

Renee stared at the white rectangle nestled beneath her refrigerator magnet and still couldn't believe it. The image had all but completely disappeared. She noted the sunlight coming through her kitchen window but didn't see that it directly aimed at the refrigerator surface. It wasn't a complete surprise, of course; she had watched the image slowly fade over the course of several months, much like the way her favorite green hook rug had faded in response to the relentless rays that pierced her office window.

She had printed the photo awhile back and couldn't really remember what kind of ink or paper she'd used. She'd just been so excited about being able to print pictures from home; the printer price was great, and the free inks seemed like a great deal at the time.

Still, she'd kept the disappearing photo in the back of her mind each time she printed new pictures to send to family. She was using newer equipment now and hoped that would solve the problem.

She worried, though, wondering whether the photos she'd printed a couple of years ago would fare better since they were tucked away in a photo album. She remembered that the pictures she'd printed for her husband to keep in his wallet had stuck to the plastic sleeving, pulling the image right off the paper. Could this be happening in that photo album?

She wasn't sure she wanted to know the answer.

One of the most wonderful aspects of digital photography is that there are a plethora of opportunities to print all your images. Sometimes it's easy, but many times it isn't. Today's digital printing technologies can reduce even the most competent person to babbling, cursing, and tears. So many choices, so many materials, and so much to learn. How do we make sure we've made the right choice — one that will ensure our prints last at least as long as prints from film do?

Ease of use aside, the availability and affordability of a personal digital darkroom has never been better.

Preserving those printed pictures is another matter.

Anyone who has watched their ink-jet photos fade, run, wash away, or stick to another page in a photo album understands this concern. After all, we printed these pictures because they were deemed important enough to make the effort. They should last for a while, shouldn't they?

You might be surprised to learn that the issue of picture fading isn't new. There have been several periods of time where people have found their

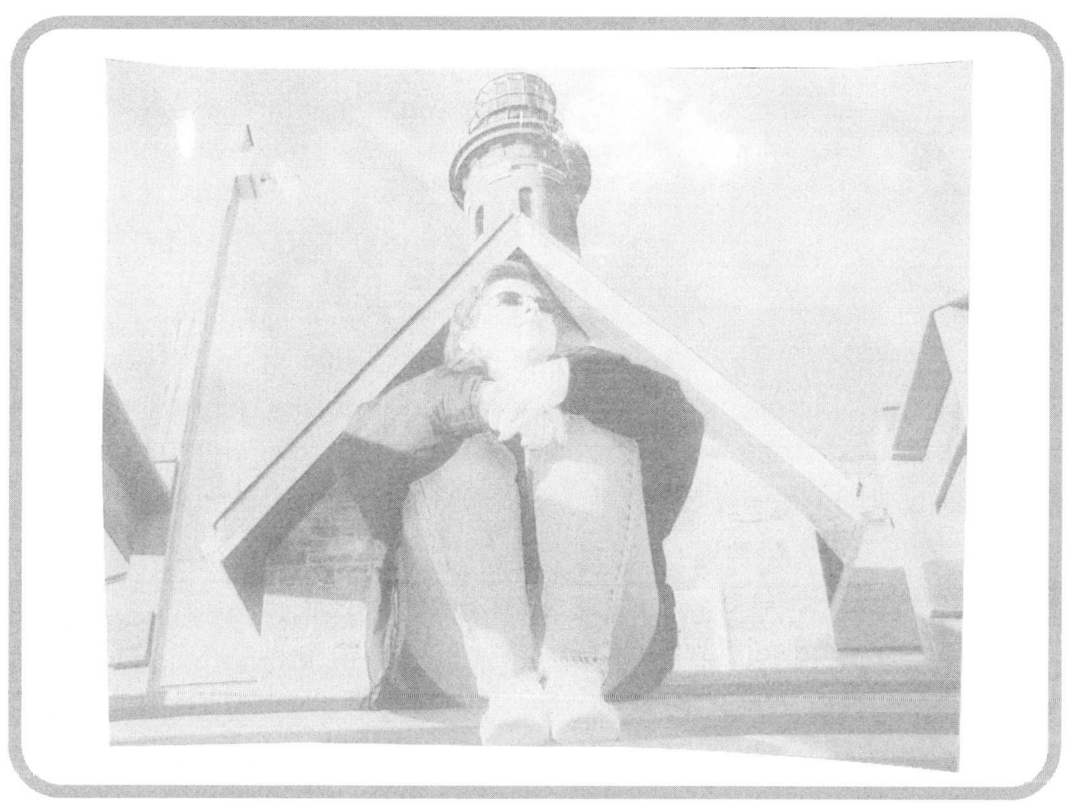

Photo 6A
While many of today's inkjet products have well tested archival qualities, some offered only a few years ago have demonstrated they can't stand the test of time. If you've printed pictures in the last three or four years, you may want to take a look at them to see how they've weathered the elements.

color photographs fading faster than the latest teen fad. Up until the 1950s, pictures were printed in black and white. If those photos were processed and handled well, they would resist many of the elements and stand the test of time. When color printing entered the market toward the end of the 1950s, people assumed that color prints would have the same longevity as their black and white predecessors.

Snapshots

Go Vertical!

Many people stick with the standard horizontal format when snapping pictures. Some photos really come into focus when switching to vertical. Consider tightening up the shot and shooting a few vertical pictures. If possible, keep the flash on top and don't let your hands or the camera strap creep into view!

Not so.

Many companies were so focused on getting their products into the market and building their customer base that few paid attention to the longevity of color photographs. It was only after twenty or thirty years had passed that people realized that color photography and the materials used (and they varied by manufacturer) didn't last as long. Many amateur pictures, professional portraits, and even important historical photographs and documents faded. Some even disappeared completely.

Only Diamonds Last Forever

A recent industry study indicated that over 70 percent of consumers think a photograph should last forever. While we agree that they should, the painful truth is that many of them won't, especially the ones printed over the last few years.

Why?

I'll spare you the in-depth exploration of the changes in digital printing technology and how they've manifested into this complicated chaos of issues but will tell you that the biggest issue we have to face today is one of standards.

Or a lack of them.

For some time, the photo industry has grappled with the issue of creating one standard for testing the image-print permanence of digitally printed photographs. Two industry associations — the International Organization for Standardization (ISO) and the American National Standards Institute (ANSI) — are working toward this goal but, at the time of printing, have not yet come to an agreement on a standardized methodology.

Okay, if you're wondering how you're supposed to figure out the best printers and inks to use when our industry can't even agree on a standard way of measuring and qualifying how long a print will last, you aren't alone. The good news is that there are some resources available and finding the best solution may be easier than you think. You just need to know where to look.

Archival Doesn't Mean Much

Many digital photography companies promote archival inks and papers, but because there is no standard, there is also no true definition of the word *archival*. What does *archival* mean? Will it last longer than your Uncle Ernie's marriage to that blackjack dealer in Vegas? What about the times you used those super cheap ink refills? Did the company promote archival inks, and if so, what company did they come from? In what year were they produced?

Unfortunately, *archival* is a term thrown around like a football in marketing materials and sales pitches, but the lack of a true standard leaves us worrying about how long our digital pictures will be around. We should worry. Put simply, if you printed your pictures a couple of years ago and can't remember the specifics of what materials you used, it's time to pull those images off your computer or CDs and print another copy.

Millions of people really are in jeopardy of losing five years of their lives. That's the way photo imaging analyst Kristy Holch, founder of InfoTrends describes what she calls "the train wreck consumers don't see coming." What she's referring to is the fact that hundreds of millions of printed images are literally fading away, and most consumers are unaware this is happening. Holch sees a real crisis on the horizon. "Our fear is that consumers will take wonderful digital photos, but those photos will be lost to future generations. Until better storage/archival solutions come along, all of today's digital photos are at risk. At InfoTrends, we feel that it's a very real possibility that there will be a 3 – 5 year gap in the personal photos of families around the world, as the photos taken between the years 2002 – 2007 are lost for lack of simple, foolproof archival mechanisms."[9]

One common issue from the early years of home printing is that most people printed their digital photos on plain white paper in an effort to save money or for convenience. "People just printed for the moment, with little thought for how long that image would actually last," states Holch. "The image looked good when it was printed, and that wonderful feeling of instant gratification overshadowed any thought of longevity. As a result, consumers have not been making informed choices on the type of paper they use or the inks."[11] Today's statistics show that we're getting savvier about using the right papers — InfoTrends indicates that, in 2005, 43 percent of prints were made on photo paper, 22 percent were on plain paper, 29 percent were on silver-halide paper, 4 percent were on dye-sublimation paper, and 1 percent were on specialty materials (such as stickers or other novelty products). The larger challenge here is to rescue the photos printed a few years ago and to make sure they are still safe in digital form, so they can be reprinted using today's superior technology.

Holch has championed this issue in the imaging industry for some time, as she worries that countless digital photographs will fade, giving consumers few options in retrieving the photographs. The issue of managing a growing library of digital photographs also contributes to this problem in that people who are printing a hard copy for backup purposes are using methods that won't stand the test of time. Some printed photographs may fade in as little as a year. Conditions including storage, light, papers, and inks used can all contribute to this issue.

"The digital files are not being well-maintained by consumers, so the print may be all they have," Holch says. "If the print is not made on long-life paper, consumers could easily lose any record of those photos in the space of just a few years." She says with concern, "Most consumers are not doing a good job of backing up their digital files."[12]

Holch recognizes that part of this issue falls to the industry she serves, but in their defense, she states, "That's because most consumers have shown little interest in this topic."[13] Some companies that cater to professional photographers or graphics designers and advanced amateurs pay more attention to this issue, but this is due in part to the fact that these users actively seek this information. After all, who wants to pay a portrait photographer hundreds or thousands of dollars for professional portraits, only to find the image on the wall is fading just a few years later? In those professions, it is critical to create a product (and photos are their product) that has permanence as its foundation. You can protect your own photographs by thinking of your images in the same light.

Snapshots

Did You Know?
Anne Geddes's strikingly beautiful photographs of children "growing" out of flower pots and resting amid the oaks have earned her a reputation as one of the most innovative and talented photographers of our generation. Although you may think she walked around with a camera as a child creating artistic images, she didn't even consider that she could make a living at photography until she was twenty-five years old.

The majority of us assume that our digital pictures will last a lifetime. This simply isn't the case; longevity requires our purposeful action.

The Expert on Your Side

Henry Wilhelm, the founder of Wilhelm Imaging Research, is considered by many as the premier expert in image-print permanence. He has conducted extensive research and countless permanence tests over his thirty-five-year career. The mere mention of his name in technology industry circles creates a knowing nod and mentions of respect for both the work and the man.

He has also recently created the Independent WIR Certified Image

Permanence testing Program and Seal, a program designed to apply standardized permanence testing and ratings to many of today's digital printing materials. Manufacturers voluntarily submit their products to the Wilhelm Institute for testing, measurement, and ranking. Wilhelm Imaging Research offers rankings and easy-to-reference tables that indicate a company's permanence rating from testing. Wilhelm created this certification program precisely because there is no current standard for testing today's digital print permanence. As someone who is passionate about the topic and works toward greater awareness toward this issue, Wilhelm has become the person many in the photo industry turn to for an understanding of topics related to how long today's pictures will last.

To learn more about Wilhelm Imaging Research, please visit www.wilhelm-research.com. Wilhelm has countless articles and papers available for free download and even offers his book *The Permanence and Care of Color Photographs: Traditional and Digital Color Prints, Color Negatives, Slides, and Motion Pictures* at no charge. The book is considered a standard reference in the industry.

Or, if you'd like, peruse his website for some of the latest articles written by computer and photography magazines on the issue. You'll be up to date on this topic and armed with the knowledge you need to make the right choice for your needs.

The issue of print permanence and archiving is even more vital for those artistic women that can transform a few digital pictures into a thoughtful chronicle of stories, creative elements, and other accents. After all, since pictures typically serve as the foundation for scrapbooks, it is critical that your photos are printed with and on materials that will stand the test of time.

Environmental Factors

Humidity, heat, and light are the major environmental factors that affect our printed photographs. Manufacturers explore these issues by using what is called accelerated testing, which essentially means that the laboratory is using specific techniques to mimic the passing of time and will make assumptions that sometimes do not reflect real-world conditions. For example, when testing photographs for issues such as heat, humidity, and light, the tests assume that the pictures are framed under glass and exposed to light for approximately twelve hours per day. Projections are then made based upon the results of the testing.

While these methods make some assumptions and actual results can vary from what is discovered and projected in the lab, they are extremely useful benchmarks to help today's digital camera users choose their printing methods from an informed standpoint. They are one of the most important road maps we have in making decisions regarding how to best protect our digital photographs.

Of all the issues that can impact your printed pictures, exposure to light remains at the head of the pack. Just look around your home for fabric-covered chairs or rugs that have been exposed to direct sunlight over time. Are the dyes fading in the exposed places?

Make sure that the inks you purchase for your printer cite specifics regarding light resistance. There are many products on the market that still do not clearly state that they have been tested for longevity. If you can't find any notation about archival qualities or resistance to elements, there's probably a reason why.

Humidity is also a factor in image fading. The term *relative humidity* (RH) indicates the volume of moisture held in materials at equilibrium with our environment. Relative humidity and temperature can affect three kinds of decay processes: mechanical, biological, and chemical. For photographs, chemical deterioration is an issue since water is considered a reactant in many decay processes, and an increase in relative humidity increases the concentration of water. Some materials will decay faster than others but the decay rates will escalate if there is an increase in relative humidity and temperature.[14]

Special Note for Scrapbookers

Scrapbooks are treasured tomes that must be carefully protected. Because of their unique and physical nature, they can be far more susceptible to fire, weather catastrophes, or environmental damage. Did you know that you can make a copy of your scrapbook?

While this process may be a bit more involved than simply scanning traditional photographs, you can take a picture of your pages to preserve them. A couple of decades ago, photo shops would use a copystand (a small piece of equipment that serves as a backdrop and has lighting attached) to take a photo of another picture, which they would write to film, process, and then use that picture for editing (such as restoring an old photograph). Today's commercial copystands can cost a few hundred dollars and may not be an option for your budget. You can, however, use a few tricks to take photographs of your scrapbook pages to preserve them for posterity.

Place your scrapbook pages on the floor and place a solid black or other solid-color cloth underneath the pages. Stay away from shiny or wrinkled material; go with simple items with no lines if at all possible. Stand over your scrapbook, frame the shot, and take a few sample pictures. You can then burn those images to disc so that you have a digital copy of your artwork.

If you prefer, you can also take your scrapbook to your local photo shop and inquire about their services. You may find their prices are competitive, and this will save you some time by handing this task over to an expert.

This process is a bit involved, but when you consider how much time, money, and energy you've invested in your scrapbook, taking the extra step to insure you've got some form of duplicate is almost as important as the scrapbook itself.

The Three Types of Digital Photo Printing Processes (or More Than You Ever Really Wanted to Know about the Subject)

Although digital photography is just now coming out of adolescence, much progress has been made in the area of digital photo printing. This is due, in part, to the fact that those in the photographic industry have placed a great deal of emphasis on the printed photograph, because it is the paper picture that has been the cash cow for film manufacturers and photo shops. As digital photography became more popular with consumers, people in the "photo space" focused their efforts on finding ways to get prints from digital cameras.

> **Snapshots**
>
> **Did You Know?**
>
> Frame Your Favorite Shots: If you want to protect your pictures from the effects of light, consider placing your favorite pictures in a frame with UV glass or in an album where they'll be spared the harsh glare of the afternoon sun.

Unfortunately, the early attempts at digital printing gave less than stellar results and even today's technologies, if not properly used, can result in a photograph with a short life span. Henry Wilhelm told Jefferson Graham of *USA Today* that while many ink-jet prints can last longer than those printed in photo labs, "If you bought a new Hewlett-Packard printer and non H-P paper, those prints... could start fading as soon as two months." Wilhelm adds that the thing to remember is: "If they (digital camera users) are thinking about even the possibility of handing them on to the next generation, they should really stay away from papers where there is no actual data available for the printer and inks they are using. Otherwise they are just flying blind."[15]

Silver-Halide Paper

Color silver-halide photo paper is used for making photos from color negative film. It is the paper our photos are printed on when we have our film processed and printed, and it has served as the standard in retail photo processing for several decades. The paper is chemically processed, and the dyes are inside the paper itself. This same paper is also used by many photo labs that offer printing of digital photographs. Such labs use a specialized machine called a digital minilab, and the equipment can cost anywhere from $100,000 - $200,000 and requires regular maintenance and some specialized training.

> **Snapshots**
>
> **For the Kids — Be Bubbly**
>
> Blowing bubbles is a great way to get infants and toddlers to look at the camera. This is best to do outside (so it doesn't stain your carpet) and keep the bubbles close to the photographer, not the child (that is, unless you want to have the bubbles in the picture!).

The benefits of using silver-halide paper are numerous. Perhaps the most important is that many of the materials used have an archive life of anywhere between 20 – 100 years. Most photo retailers are quite careful about their choice of materials, but there are variances in any industry, so don't hesitate to ask if you are unsure. Some photo retailers also often employ the latest in digital color management and have technologies that are capable of auto-correcting photographs, delivering a high-quality printed picture without requiring you to do anything to create that result outside of handing over your digital camera card or CD.

Make sure to ask about the kinds of materials they are using to print your photographs. If they know you understand the issue of image permanence, they'll likely take that into account in deciding which materials they choose to use in their equipment.

Dye Sublimation

The second type of digital photo paper commonly used is called dye sublimation, a technology that is also used often in retail locations and spe-

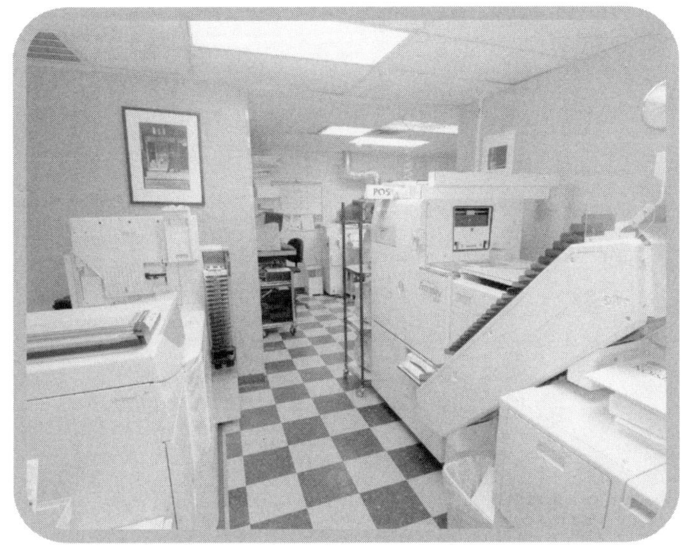

Photo 6B
Many of today's photo retailers print your digital pictures using specialized equipment called digital minilabs, or DMLs, that are designed to use the same materials you were accustomed to receiving with your 35mm film photographs.

cialty shops. They are often found in the photo kiosks you use in your favorite drugstore or specialty shop.

Commonly referred to as *dye sub*, this printer format has also been used in some home printing models, although the price points demonstrate they are best suited for small businesses, graphic designers, photographers, or others capable of spending several hundred to several thousand dollars on a printer. In this process, a separate dye sheet of each color — cyan, magenta, yellow, and the printer puts the three colors together to make black — is used to produce a full color print. Heat is applied to the color sheet, and the dye is transferred to the paper, resulting in a color photograph. The paper often feels a bit thinner than silver-halide paper, although today's latest models make it difficult to tell the difference between the two.

Early dye-sublimation printers did not have a protective layer guarding against fading and fingerprints. Photographs printed on these models are

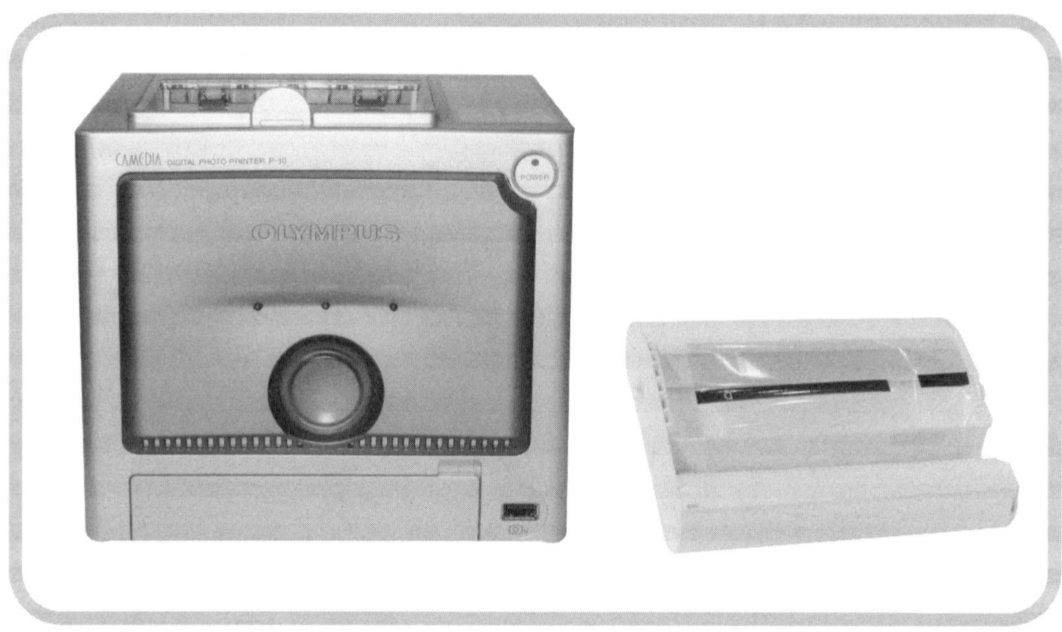

Photos 6C & 6D
Dye sublimation printers are another way of printing your digital pictures and are often used in photo kiosks found at your local retail shop or drug store. Some companies now offer home models for those wanting an alternative to inkjet printers. Unlike ink jet printers, dye sublimation printers use a special ribbon to transfer the photographic image onto the paper.

likely to exhibit some image degradation already. Today's dye sublimation technologies — used in both home and retail applications — now have a protective coating to enhance image life.

Ink-Jet Inks and Printers

Probably the most commonly used method of printing digital camera images is ink-jet printing. Ink-jet technology has advanced in many respects over the last several years, and executives from companies such as Epson and HP say that today's ink-jet technologies can match the longevity of pictures printed on

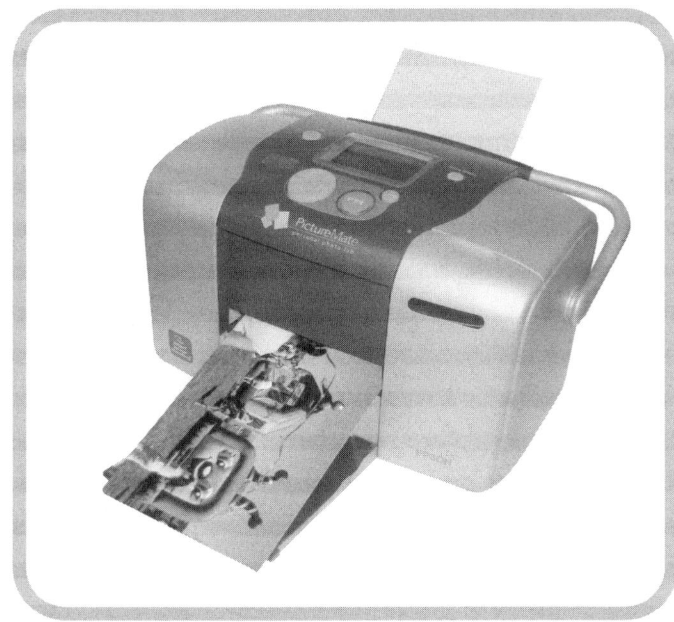

Photo 6E
Today's top ink jet printers boast many features and materials designed to better stand up to environmental factors such as heat and light.

traditional silver-halide materials. There are some studies that back up this contention, which can mean great benefits for those who enjoy printing at home.

Nevertheless, caveat emptor is still the rule when it comes to choosing ink-jet printers, papers, and inks. There are basically two types of inks: dye-based inks using dyes similar to those found in color silver-halide papers and pigment-based inks. Most ink-jet printers today use dye-based inks, since they offer the widest range of colors most people need to create high-quality color photographs. Pigment-based inks, however, have better lasting qualities in terms of weathering the elements of light. Still, both options can yield the results you're looking for as long as you follow a few guidelines.

For selecting ink-jet papers, make sure to use a paper that is coated to accept the inks rather than using uncoated paper, which will simply allow the inks to rest on the surface. Of course, one of the exciting things about early generations of photo printers was that you could use regular typing or copy paper. Unfortunately, those papers aren't designed to create photographic-quality prints.

The three types of ink-jet printing papers available are swellable paper, porous paper, and cotton-rag paper. The term *swellable* is derived from the fact that the coating is able to swell to two or three times the original thickness as it absorbs the ink. Once the coating has absorbed all of the ink, the paper returns to its original thickness.

Swellable papers are non-porous; they should be used with dye-based inks that are absorbed into the paper. If used with pigmented inks, the inks may sit on the surface and not take full advantage of either the ink or the paper. In addition, swellable papers can be affected by moisture, fingerprints, and even aerosol sprays.

The top surface of a porous paper is coated with microscopic inert particles that create cavities into which ink is deposited. These cavities keep the ink from spreading and help to make the paper dry faster. Porous papers work better with pigmented inks rather than dye-based inks since the pigmented inks have better light-keeping properties.

Cotton-based papers, called cotton rag, are manufactured to some of the best archival specifications. These papers are usually acid- and lignin-free. When used with pigmented inks, these will have the longest overall print life.

Many of today's manufacturers offer products that are rated for light-fastness, so check the back of the package for indications of a specific rating.

Do I Really Need to Use What the Manufacturers Suggest?

With so many alternatives on the market today for photo paper and inks — refillable cartridges and generic branded accessories — it is a common practice to purchase materials based solely upon price. In the photo industry, inks and paper are referred to as consumables, or "razor blades,"

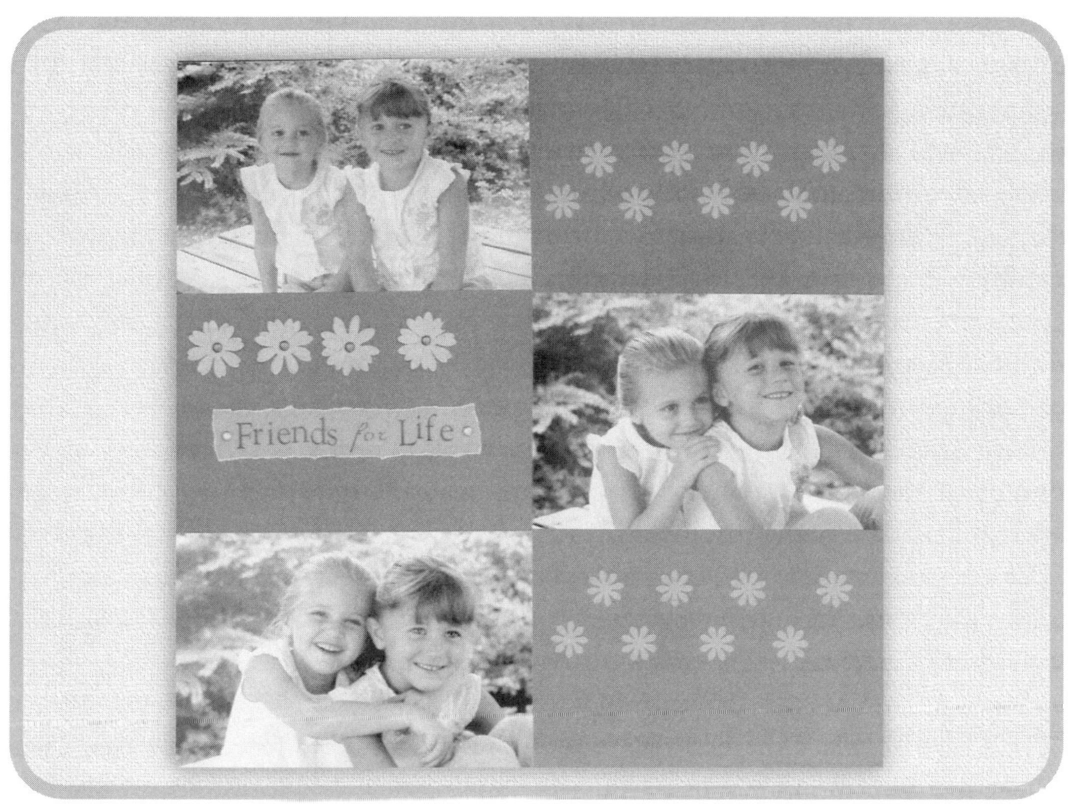

Photo 6F
Scrapbookers need to pay special attention to the materials used in printing their photos. These books are often intended to be passed along to loved ones, so archival materials are critical.

meaning that they sell the printers at a very low profit margin and make their money on the refill items. Many people experience a bit of sticker shock when going to their local office supply store or consumer electronics store to purchase ink cartridges, and it turns out the cost per print is sometimes higher than expected. With those factors in play, it makes sense that we would want to print at the lowest price possible.

That said, if you want your photos to stand up against time and the elements, follow the manufacturer's guidelines, even if the price is a bit higher. It's worth it. Today's color printer manufacturers are increasingly sensitive to the issues of image permanence and spend substantial research and development dollars improving both their papers and their inks. In order to achieve the optimum results the manufacturer has experienced in its own testing labs, following their guidelines is the best way to achieve that goal. A little extra money is worth the peace of mind, especially if you are using the printed photographs as backup for your computer images, for scrapbooks, for display, or as gifts.

Some studies also find that if you use paper termed *archival* but that is not manufactured by the same company as the printer being used, you can end up with pictures that fade in as little as a few years. While the ratings and quality will continue to improve, it is extremely important to remember that each company is working to maximize longevity using its own ink and paper products, so if longevity is important to you, follow the guidelines to the letter.

What about Ink Refills?

There are a number of companies that promote how much money can be saved by recycling ink cartridges and having them refilled. There seem to be a number of reasons to do this, including the ability to recycle and the substantial cost savings that can occur from using ink refill companies.

If you're going to start using a service such as this, it's extremely important to ask what kind of inks are being used and if they have the archival qualities of being resistant to light, heat, and other elements. If possible, you need to also find out what year the inks were manufactured. Today's ink-jet technologies are tremendously better than those available even a couple of years ago, but some of these companies use the cheapest materials. If you go this route, do so at your own risk.

If you're using ink refills for printed pictures, verify what's going into the cartridge. If you aren't sure, take your picture outside in the sun and leave it there for a few days. If it fades, it's time to reconsider.

Kim Newton, an MBA, mother of two, and avid scrapbooker residing in Houston, Texas, remembers a time when she'd sent an ink-jet photo to a family member. "My mother-in-law had put the picture on her refrigerator. It wasn't even in the direct sunlight, but it didn't take long for the picture to turn completely white. It just dissolved."

Outside Solutions

Retail Stores

Today's photo shops little resemble the ones you may have frequented ten or twenty years ago. Gone are the loud and clunky box-shaped machines spitting out 4 x 6 prints from film while the fragrance of chemicals lingered in the air. The sheer number of specialty shops has declined tremendously — there are fewer than 8,000 independent photo stores in the United States today — but there are more retail stores offering photo services than ever before. Most drugstores have a dedicated photo counter, and many supermarkets are following suit; even many consumer electronics stores and office supply stores are now offering digital printing services.

With this proliferation of retail photo services comes increased benefits for digital camera users. One increasingly popular fixture in these shops is known as a photo kiosk. Getting prints and other services from your digital camera card is often as simple as inserting your digital camera card into the unit, touching the screen, and following the instructions. These systems have been in photo stores since 1995 — the early models from companies such as Eastman Kodak and Pixel Magic Imaging scanned photographs rather than taking digital camera images (and are still in operation today) — and today's digital photo kiosks are extremely simple to use.

Many allow you to use your credit card or pay the cashier for the pho-

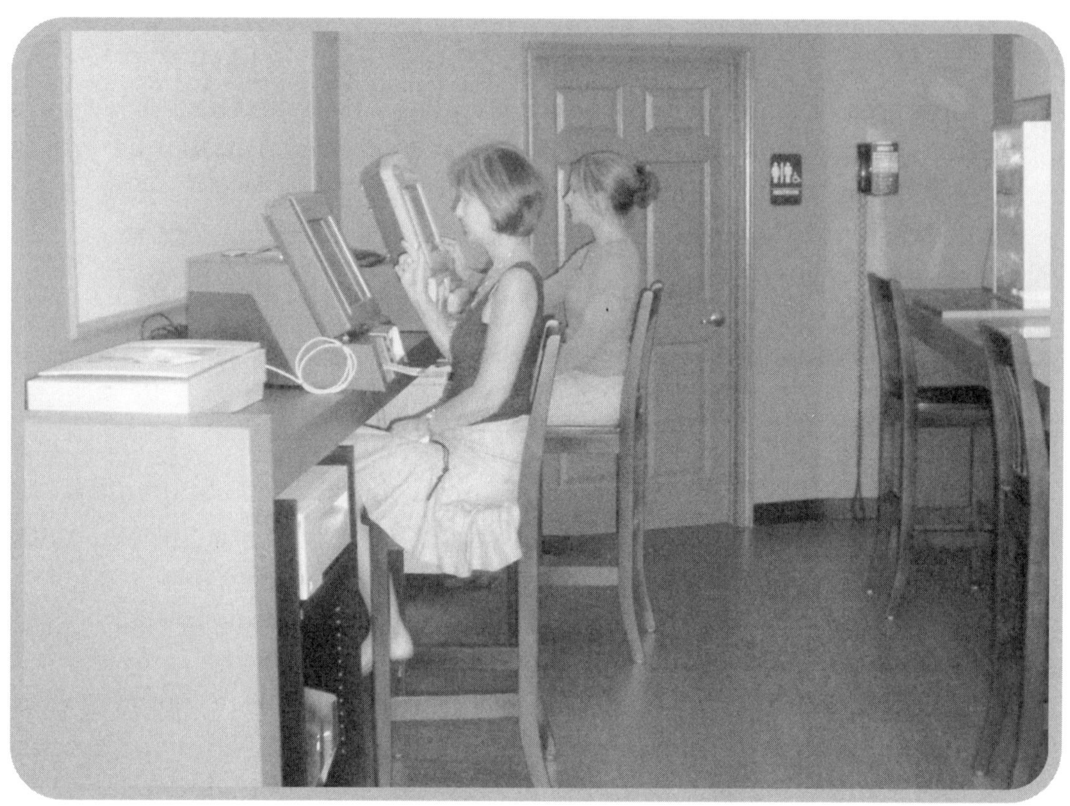

Photo 6G
Some retailers now offer kiosk cafés for those wanting to spend a bit of time enhancing their images. Many even have activities to entertain the kids while you work.

tographs, and if you wish to let the photo lab personnel handle the order, you can simply ask them for help or leave your camera card for them to fulfill the order in much the same way your film orders were filled. If you're wary of leaving your camera card in someone else's care, burn the images on a CD before going to the store.

Many find using a photo kiosk to be a great deal of fun because there are so many things you can do with the photographs. Some stores now offer kiosk cafés where you can sit with a cup of coffee and work on your digital pictures; many even have play areas for those with small children.

Today's photo kiosks offer all kinds of services from automatic red-eye removal to color balance to special effects, such as turning color photographs into black and white or sepia. Many of these kiosks also offer CD archiving and specialty products such as calendars, announcements, or even photo books.

Most kiosks used in photo shops or drugstores print to a digital minilab using silver-halide paper or dye-sublimation printers. Many use multiple methods so that they may offer instant delivery, one-hour, or next-day service. If you have any doubts, simply ask about the archival qualities of the paper used. Today's generation of silver-halide paper is considered archival in most forms, but again, asking your photo technician to verify this fact will give great peace of mind. If you don't get a straight answer or feel that the employee doesn't really understand the issue, don't hesitate to ask for a manager or the store owner. Like most businesses, many retail stores have a regular turnover of staff, and sometimes you need to reach a manager or shop owner to get the information you need.

Online Companies

Most online companies now mimic the equipment chosen by retail photo stores — specifically using digital minilabs — since they are, in essence, a photo store that provides their services over the Internet. There are countless companies offering digital printing, and it is more difficult to tell much about the company since you can't walk into their store and examine the operation. Going with a well-known company, such as a brand name you already trust or a referral from a friend, is a great way to start, but you'll still want to verify the company uses archival materials. Simply check their website or send an email to their customer service team to verify the use of archival materials.

The Big Picture

Regardless of the method you choose — printing at home, printing online, printing at a photo shop, or a combination of all three — a little research will go a long way when it comes to protecting your printed photographs. When you open your photo album thirty years from now to reminisce with children or grandchildren, it is far more likely the images will be in top condition to enjoy or pass down to loved one. That knowledge alone is worth a few extra pennies and minutes spent.

- Locate any photographs you may have printed during the years 2000 and later to check their condition. If you can find the images on your computer or on disc, flag those images for reprinting and storage, noting on the back the year it was printed. Make sure you can still find and open the files.

- If you're purchasing a printer, verify it uses archival inks and check the specifics regarding water and light resistance. Look for specific data detailing how long the manufacturer estimates the materials will last.

- Visit the Wilhelm Imaging Research website at www.wilhelm-research.com to learn the testing results of some of your favorite digital printers and paper.

- If your current ink-jet printer doesn't offer archival inks and papers, consider using a specialty photo store or drugstore for printing those photographs you want to protect or use that money to invest in a newer ink-jet printer that does use archival materials. Make sure to ask your local photo retailer about the kinds of materials they use and request the specific archival data (e.g., seventy-five years).

- Use digital printing as one key method of backing up photos but not the only one. Remember your redundancy plan (two backups on two formats in two locations).

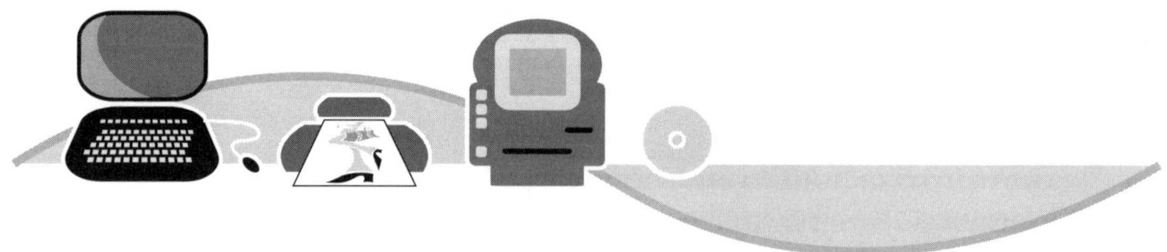

7

Smile

For the Camera Phone!

Lisa's life was a bit like a sitcom in that it seemed she was forever a victim of orchestrated mayhem. Her four children had more social engagements than Laura Bush, and she always forgot something of importance each time she loaded up her car to run an errand or take one of her kids to what felt like an endless stream of athletic events. Goldfish crackers crunched under foot, and every week meant finding something suspiciously similar to a kind of snack food growing underneath one of her car seats. While she'd regularly forget sporting gear, important paperwork, or even her first name at times, at least she'd never forgotten one of her kids!

She would also never forget her cell phone. It was her lifeline to managing the countless details of her life. It was her American Express card; she never left home without it.

One of the things that frustrated her most was the fact that, while she'd been witness to so many great events in her children's lives, she had almost no photos to chronicle the events or to save for them when they got older. Her digital camera almost always remained tucked in its carrying case in a desk drawer. Listening to her friends talk about their elaborate scrapbooks made her wince; she could never remember to bring her camera, let alone print the images and adorn them in an aesthetic way for posterity.

Just when she thought all was lost, she discovered the camera phone. She would no longer be burdened with the guilt of forgetting her camera because she always had her cell phone with her. The euphoria was short-lived, however. It wouldn't take long for Lisa to realize that her camera phone wasn't quite as simple as she'd hoped. Sure, she could take a picture. But she couldn't figure out how to send them to other people or how to get them off the phone and onto her computer. Adding insult to injury, she learned that her carrier would charge her for every picture she took and sent across their network. She had to pay to get access to her own pictures!

She'd also been warned by a friend that camera phones only took "throw-away" pictures and that they wouldn't be good enough to print. Not one to rely only on the opinion of others, Lisa decided to test it for herself. Sure enough, the pictures were fuzzy and dark — nowhere near the quality she'd come to expect from her digital camera.

Suddenly, the camera phone became yet another source of frustration at a time when Lisa thought she'd finally found the solution to her picture-taking problems.

If you don't own a camera phone, you've probably seen the advertisements on television. Unfortunately, they usually involve teenagers snapping obnoxious photos of their friends and then broadcasting them to the entire student population just for laughs.

"Today's advertisements aren't doing a very good job of promoting the benefits of camera phones,"[16] says Alan Reiter, a top wireless technologies analyst who has covered the industry for twenty-six years. Reiter sees a world where people increasingly carry scores of photos *and* videos with them on their cell phones rather than keeping hard copy photos in a wallet. He sees real estate agents transmitting images to clients, construction workers taking photos of problems onsite and asking supervisors for advice. He knows EMS professionals are now taking pictures of accident scenes and immediately transferring the images to the hospital or to get a doctor to a site. More than anything, he sees countless possibilities and points to the fact that people around the world are already discovering new ways to use camera phones.

Reiter has probably forgotten more about this technology than most of us could ever remember. His enthusiasm for the wireless industry is impossible to ignore; his comments pour out like a water fountain and his thoughts often divert like side streets, only to reconnect with a central point and shed new light on an existing topic.

It seems that Reiter's enthusiasm is contagious, and many of us are ready to trade in last year's phone models for new ones with the ability to snap photographs and make phone calls. And the United States is still a far cry from where Japan is in relation to mobile phones, although the gap is closing. In the Japanese market, it is getting increasingly difficult to purchase a cell phone that *doesn't* have a camera lens built into the handset.

Why all the focus on camera phones? In part, the popularity of digital photography itself has helped camera phones evolve, because much of the research conducted for digital cameras can also be leveraged by the cell

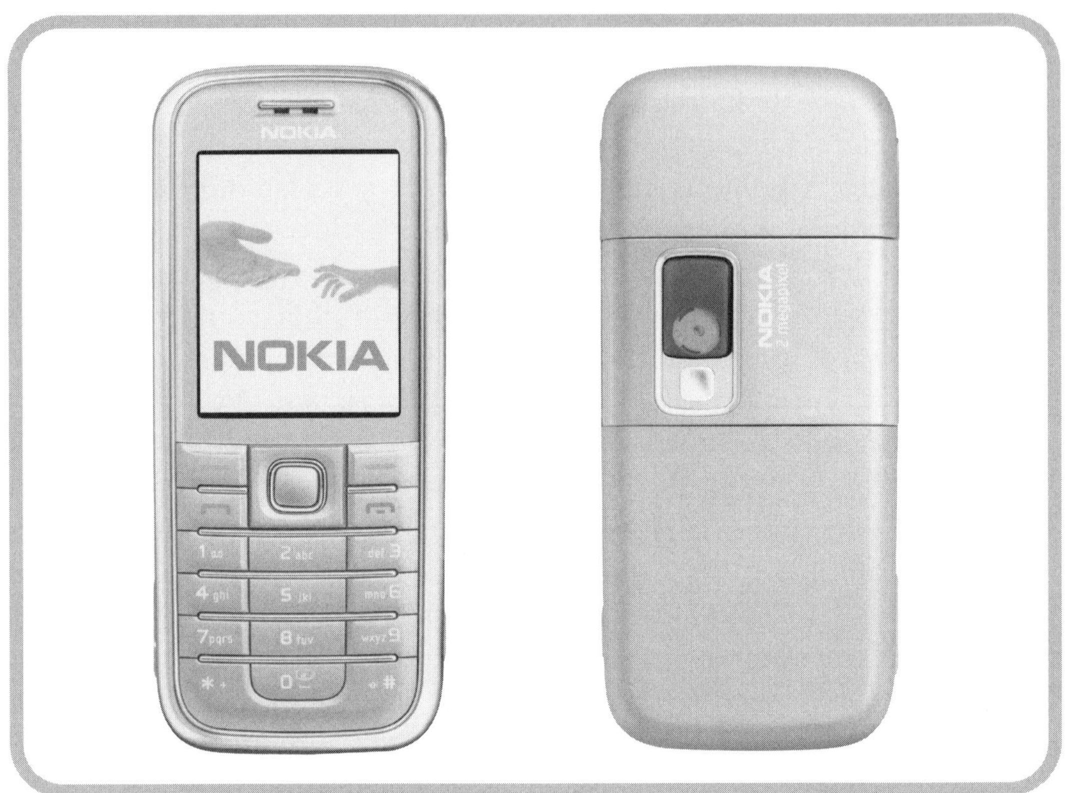

Photo 7A
While the camera phone may not replace your digital camera anytime soon, it can be extremely handy for those times you find yourself without any other way of capturing an important moment. Today's camera phones continue to improve their image quality, proving themselves to be nice complements to higher end digital cameras. *Photo courtesy of Nokia.*

phone manufacturers. Pictures are a method of communication, so it makes sense to many to have a digital camera built into a cell phone. We can already surf the Web, manage our calendars, and customize our ring tones, so a camera lens may be the latest addition to a Swiss army knife sort of communication device. The wireless industry — people who make

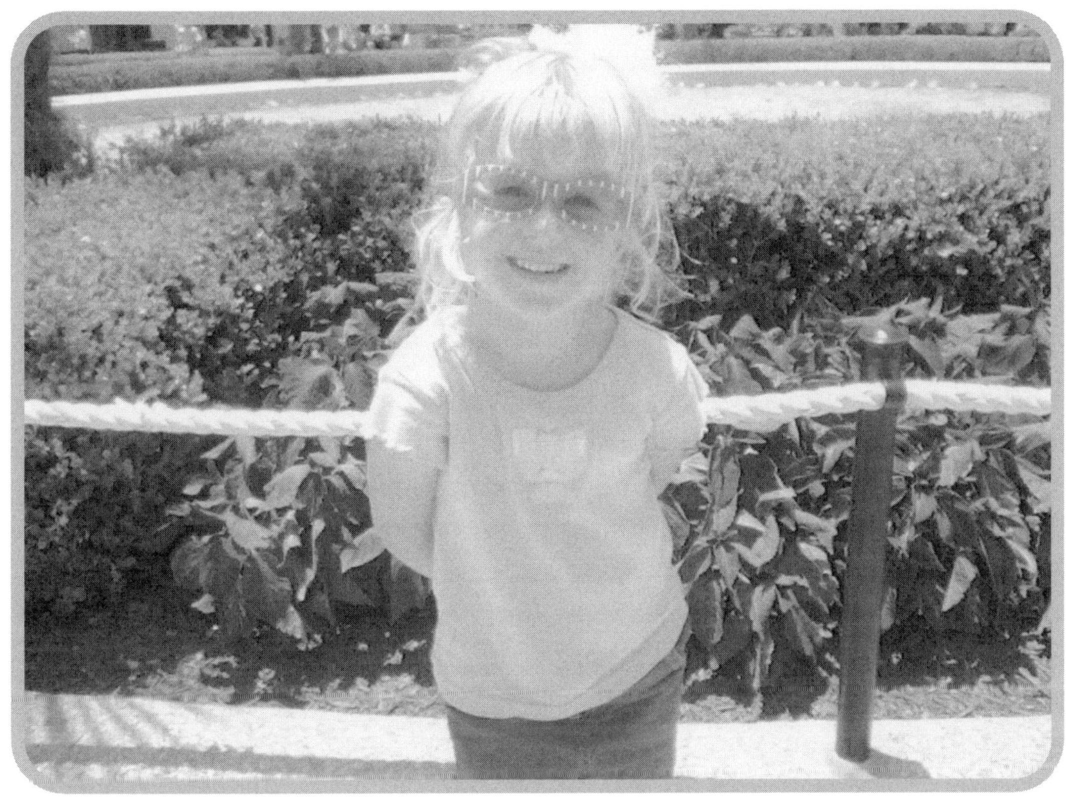

Photo 7B
This shot, captured using my camera phone, was taken to chronicle my daughter's summer visit to a local theme park. Without my phone, I wouldn't have this shot, and it is one of my favorites to this day.

the handsets, write the software, and provide wireless service — see camera phones as a way to make more money and are paying careful attention to how the public uses these devices.

Will Camera Phones Replace Digital Cameras Soon?

People in the digital photography and communications industries deal with this question on a daily basis, and it appears that there is no real consensus on the answer. One of the leading research organizations, InfoTrends, issued a release in January of 2005 stating that it projected worldwide camera phone sales would grow from 178 million units in 2004 to over 860 million units in 2009. This research group and some of its industry peers agree that almost 90 percent of all mobile phone handsets shipped by 2009 will include a camera lens as part of the basic design.

This doesn't mean camera phones will simply replace digital cameras. Many industry experts believe digital cameras will still dominate, but camera phones will be an additional camera, to be used when the primary camera is forgotten or not available. The digital camera will be the primary picture-taking device because of the high-quality images it creates; today's breed of digital cameras do so much to help us take beautiful pictures, and the camera phone would be hard pressed to compete on that level. But camera phones will be great for immediate and impromptu situations. In essence, if you forgot your camera, no worries, just whip out your cell phone! And, of course, many of us already do just that.

Camera phones still have a long way to go in terms of rivaling the picture quality and experience of using today's top digital cameras. Features such as flash and zoom contribute greatly to the ability to take a high-quality photograph; these features are now becoming available on camera phones, but they still have a long way to go due to size and cost constraints. Even the way camera phones must be held affects the kinds of shots you can take.

Still, we shouldn't discount the likelihood that camera phones will continue to get better with time. Just a few years ago, many in the photo industry felt that digital cameras would be nothing more than a gadget and film would continue to reign as the picture-taking medium of choice. Industry experts believe that both camera phones and digital cameras will continue to evolve and provide better image quality. I expect that camera phones and digital cameras will prove to complement rather than compete with one another and that one design will not completely replace the other.

For high-quality shots of important events, the digital camera will be most popular, but if you ever forget your camera, you'll have your phone with you. You'll still have pictures and will enjoy them immensely.

> **Snapshots**
>
> **It's in the Bag!**
>
> Your digital camera is an investment that will yield years of happy memories. Protect it by investing a few dollars in a quality camera bag. Don't fear that you'll have to carry a bulky, black bag. Today's camera bags come in a range of sizes and price ranges, and many companies now offer contemporary designs for today's discriminating woman.

What to Look for in a Camera Phone

Does anyone buy a cell phone to call people anymore?

If you're shopping specifically for a phone with a camera built in, you'll likely find an experience that is both frustrating and exciting. Camera phones are evolving much faster than most industry experts expected. In fact, in Asia, it is now possible to purchase an eight-megapixel camera phone with a zoom lens and a relatively powerful flash. Before you buy, though, don't forget to consider the other ways you'll be using the phone. For example, do you like the interface? Do you like how the unit displays information? Do you feel you can navigate the menus with just a little practice, or does it feel as though you've got to whip out the manual every time you dial a number?

When some people purchase their phones, they consider the camera to be an add-on — in other words, they don't pay too much attention outside of the fact that the unit can actually take a picture. Once you have the unit and learn to use it, however, you may find yourself using the camera more often, and you will want to make sure you've got the right fit for your needs.

There are a number of important issues to consider when purchasing a camera phone. Let's take a look at them.

Resolution

While resolution isn't the sole predictor of image quality, in camera phones it is important, especially if you want to print these photos in the future. Many entry model camera phones, especially those thrown in or given away as part of a service promotion, are likely to be VGA models. VGA is 640 x 480 pixels, and this works fine if you want to simply share the images electronically. However, if you want to print the pictures, you'll want to consider a higher-resolution camera.

All the resolution in the world isn't going to make much difference if your camera lens is dirty, so remember to keep your camera phone clean. Cell phones are handled a lot more than standard digital cameras. Grease from your hands, face, and hair can be easily transferred to the camera lens, reducing sharpness, and the viewing screen, making it harder to see the image. Be careful to use a soft cloth, lens cleaning cloth, or tissue.

Memory Cards

Most of the early model camera phones did not include removable media cards as part of the handset. Some industry insiders speculate that carriers don't want consumers to be able to simply take the images off a card and download them into their computers. Many carriers charge users each time they transmit a digital picture across the network, so every time you email yourself or a friend a photo, it's going to cost you. If you have a removable media card, that money-making opportunity is lost to the carriers.

While this debate continues, more models are coming out with removable media cards. Some phones have memory cards, but they are located underneath the battery, making it a bit more cumbersome to retrieve. If possible, look for a phone that has an easily accessible media slot.

Smart phones, or phones that have PDA functions, often *require* a removable media card, because they need to hold more information than is available on the handset's internal memory. Higher megapixel camera phones create larger files, so having a media card will become even more important as the technology improves. Higher resolution pictures simply take up more space.

It would be wise to consider having a removable media slot as part of your camera phone requirements list. It will not only help you save on transmission charges, it will also make integrating your camera phone pictures into your master digital picture library much easier.

> **Snapshots**
>
> **For the Kids — Be Quick**
>
> Try having someone else behind you holding her hand over your head to get the kids to look at the camera. Let her make funny hand movements to keep the kids laughing. Take several pictures in quick succession. You can check each picture to make sure eyes are all open and such, but not too often or you'll lose your audience. Try to finish *before* everyone starts to fuss.

Flash

Some of today's models now come with a built-in flash, which helps in low-light conditions. While the flash in a camera phone may not hold a candle to the flash on your digital camera, it may improve the picture a bit, and with camera phones, every bit helps.

Bluetooth or IR

If you want to be able to send pictures wirelessly to other devices such as a computer, another cell phone (short range), a PDA, a home printer, or a retail digital printing kiosk, you'll need to have Bluetooth and/or IR (Infrared) capability.

Verify Any Tricky Transfers

Some models promote the ability to download information via Bluetooth, IR, or by using a cable that connects to your computer, but this sometimes refers to downloading contact information (names and addresses) and not photographs. The ability to download pictures and other files has been disabled. Make sure you can download *all* files off the camera or this could add up to increased charges.

Compatibility

When choosing your camera phone, ask about which companies support the model you wish to purchase. You'll want to delve carefully into their requirements regarding contracts, transmission speed, and how they bill for digital photo transmission (called MMS or multimedia messaging). Remember that many of these companies make money on transmission time, so the more pictures you take, the more money they make. Remember the removable media card!

I've Got Pictures — Now What?

Getting your digital pictures off your camera phone can be a bit confusing or frustrating at times. But much of that frustration may simply come from learning a new piece of technology, and unfortunately, some camera phones are better designed than others. There are a few things to know about accessing your camera phone pictures — and that's why you're reading this chapter!

MMS or Multimedia Messaging

Essentially, MMS is just a way to send an email with a photo, video, or audio file attached. Many of today's camera phones will let you attach audio to a photo and send it as a multimedia message. For parents who travel or for those who have loved ones far away, sending an MMS message is a great way to share photos and audio of a child's birthday message or some other special communication. Today, most carriers will let you share MMS messages across different networks. Previously, one carrier would only support MMS within its own network, so if you used one carrier and your mother used another, you wouldn't be able to share MMS messages, but consumer demand has prevailed and we are all grateful for that!

Emailing Photos

You can email yourself pictures or email them to others. If you want to share your pictures with others, you may want to have another email address set up just for this purpose. You may find you want to share photos between phones directly, and this works well. You will find it handy to have the email addresses installed in your phone's memory ahead of time. It will take a few minutes, but it is time well spent. Of course, if you have a removable media card, you may want to wait until you get home, upload the pictures using your image management software, and then send them at a later date (saving on transmission charges).

Snapshots

Did You Know?
The two million dollar question — in 1912, George Eastman, founder of Eastman Kodak, donated $2.5 million dollars to MIT (Massachusetts Institute of Technology). The only condition? No one could know he was the donor. The donation was originally said to have come from a Mr. Smith.

Printing Your Camera Phone Pictures

The quality of the camera in your phone will largely determine whether or not you'll want to print the pictures. If you have a VGA (640 x 480) camera, you may be able to get a wallet size print (2 ½ x 3 ½), and if you have an SVGA (800 x 600) camera, you might be able to print a 3 ½ x 5 photograph. To print a quality 4 x 6 print, you'll need at least 1.3 megapixels, and to print a 5 x 7 enlargement, you'll want at least a two-megapixel model.

There are a number of printing options for you to consider:

- **Printing at home.** You can print using your computer to a home ink-jet printer, or if you have a removable media card, insert it directly into a printer that supports removable media, bypassing the computer altogether. However, if it is a picture you care about, it's best to transfer the picture to your image management software first.

- **Online printing.** You can upload the images and use an online photo sharing and printing service (See chapter 5 on online services). Many of these companies offer high-quality prints (if the picture is high-quality) and also offer other novelty services.

- **Digital photo kiosks.** Digital photo kiosks are becoming increasingly popular. In addition to traditional retail settings, you can also find them on cruise ships, in airports, and in amusement parks. Many of these digital photo kiosks can print directly from your removable media card, and an increasing number are Bluetooth- and IR-enabled. Just point your camera toward the kiosk (with an IR model — with Bluetooth, no pointing necessary), touch a button or two, and the images will be loaded onto the kiosk for you to review and print.

- **File size reduction.** MMS reduces the size of the images. If you want to save your photos, offload your images from the removable media or use Bluetooth or IR.

Special Considerations for Business Owners

Like any emerging technology, camera phones can be used for good or evil. It has been reported that camera phones have been used to prevent crimes or to document a license plate or other important evidence at a crime scene. Camera phones can also be a tool for intellectual property theft. An increasing number of government agencies, military bases, and research companies are banning camera phones from their facilities, because it is so simple to snap a picture of confidential information.

If you run a business and are worried about intellectual property theft, you may wish to explore ways to better monitor these units in your business. While completely banning them or monitoring their use every second is practically impossible, you can protect yourself in some respects.

For example, if your employees use company-paid cell phones, consider getting models that do not have cameras. If they do have camera lenses built into the handset, occasionally monitor the usage (check your bills to see what pictures are being sent and to whom) from your service provider to insure your company property is being properly used.

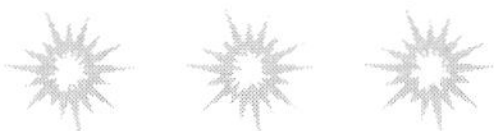

When purchasing a camera phone, consider how you intend to access and use your digital pictures. Take a look at your current habits and think about how often you intend to rely upon your camera phone as a digital camera in addition to using its traditional calling features.

I believe it is best to spend a bit more up front on resolution and memory cards because they will yield more control and cost-saving benefits in the future, but price will always be a consideration when purchasing a camera phone. As Warren Buffett once said, "Price is what you pay. Value is what you get."

Only you can determine the value you receive from your purchase.

The Big Picture

If you're in the market for a new phone, consider a camera phone instead of the freebie that the service provider offers. Once you start using it, you'll be surprised at how often you come to rely upon it in certain situations. You may also find another great way to communicate with your kids — not just with words but with pictures, too. For those parents who have kids away at college, a camera phone is a great way to stay connected.

- Today's breed of camera phones are a great complement to your high-quality digital camera. For those instances when you forget your camera, having a camera phone can help you capture that great shot that would otherwise be lost.

- There is a wide range of quality camera phones on the market. If you want to take pictures that you intend to keep over time, consider going with a higher resolution model that has a flash.

- Many of today's camera phone images can be printed at home or at a retail photo kiosk. While the image quality will likely not rival your digital camera, small pictures may be satisfactory for your purposes. Like most technology, this product category will continue to improve over time.

- Check to see if your camera phone can store pictures on a removable media card or if they can only be transmitted. Service providers charge a fee for every transmission, so consider getting a model that has a removable media card so that you can more easily import your pictures into your existing image library.

- If you are a business owner or handle sensitive information, consider what policies you need to have in place regarding camera phones in order to protect that information.

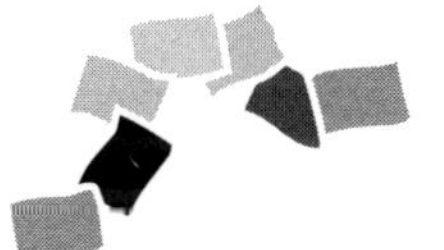

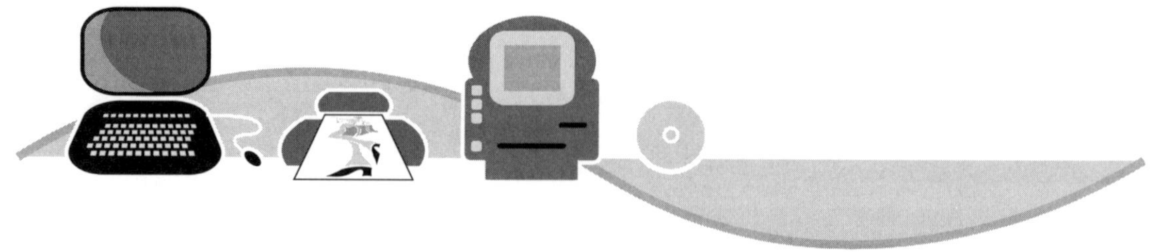

8

When All Seems Lost

Image Recovery

AS Susan entered her Spanish-style kitchen to retrieve her morning coffee, she passed the computer nestled in the area she affectionately called her private office. It was hardly private — her husband and three children regularly traipsed through the space since it was, essentially, little more than a hallway between the kitchen and the garage. Still, she took comfort that it was her own oasis, a place she entrusted to track bills, permission slips, and other stray pieces of paper sure to require attention sometime soon.

Susan placed her cup of coffee on a coaster next to her computer and slid into her chair. She waited for the computer to boot up, but the hard drive was noisy and making a grinding sound. Her pulse quickened as the monitor greeted her with a blue screen and an error with the word fatal *as part of the description. The machine locked up, giving no entry to its contents.*

"Oh no," she whispered as she frantically pounded her keyboard, moved her mouse, and attempted to re-boot her computer. She'd been meaning to back up her photographs but simply hadn't had the time with all the daily demands of running a home business and a household. Three years of her family's lives were chronicled in pictures on that computer. It was all there — her son's soccer season, her daughter's tae kwon do events, her husband's recent fishing trip, and her girlfriends' weekend backpacking trip through the mountains.

She wondered if the pictures could be retrieved or if they were lost forever. The latter was too painful to contemplate.

There are few things more unnerving than realizing your hard drive could be grinding your favorite photographs as though they were your morning coffee beans. What is even more unnerving, though, is that most people use their hard drives as a permanent storage device when experts know that a hard drive is one of the least safe places to keep important information.

Consequently, it's reasonable to expect that at some time you may sit with a system and drive that has failed. If you find yourself in this position in front of your computer with panic filling your heart because your trusted CPU has proven itself less than worthy of that trust, take heart. You are among millions who have walked this path and have been able to save their photos from permanent demise. Life as you know it has not come to an end.

A Different Kind of Corruption

Technology doesn't improve with age; rather, it often becomes cranky and less reliable. Hard drives store their information magnetically in sectors, and over time, these sectors go bad and become unreadable. When the hard drive attempts to access that particular sector, it causes problems and can force the system to crash. Electronic failures inside the system itself can also cause hard drives to die an untimely death.

Hard drive failures can either be considered physical or logical. A physical failure means that something has actually happened to the hardware itself and the result can be electrical damage or mechanical defect. As hard drive capacity explodes, the consequences of catastrophic failure mushroom. Hard drives now store not just documents but photos, music, and video. These are electronically embedded on a platter spinning at 10,000 revolutions a minute (300 times the speed of an LP), and the information is accessed by a read/write head floating just above the disc. The head mechanism travels back and forth across the disc at 60 miles per hour. If the head falls (crashes) on the platter or picks up a sub-micron of dust, the data can be rendered unreadable.

If the hard drive has suffered logical damage, it means that there can be content damage to the file system or the operating software. This can be the result of inadvertently deleting important files that the computer needs to function. It can also be caused by a computer virus or possibly an electrostatic charge. Your hard drive may still be recognized by the BIOS (which stands for Basic Input-Output System). The BIOS is the program that recognizes all your devices when your computer first boots up.

Not every hard drive file can be recovered, but most can. Sometimes as much as 90 – 95 percent of the data can be recovered.

Symptoms of Hard Drive Failure

It is important to diagnose if your computer is experiencing a true hard drive failure or if it is suffering from a less critical illness. Here is some diagnostic information, courtesy of American Data Recovery (www.adrdatarecovery.com) and is reproduced with the company's permission:

- **A clicking hard drive.** This can indicate a head crash, corrupt firmware on the drive's ROM chip, an electrical problem like a burned chip, blown heads, a bad PCB controller, overwritten servos, damage to the hard drive's platters, alignment issues from being dropped or jarred, or a power surge.

- **System blue screens.** When your system "blue screens" when you try to boot or during the middle of an operation, it can mean the operating system has been damaged, there may be bad sectors on your hard drive that the system is unable to read, your hard drive could be failing, you might have a virus or Trojan, someone may have deleted critical DLLs or system files, or the partition or file structure may have become corrupted or damaged.

- **Drive not formatted.** A "drive not formatted" error usually indicates the hard drive's partition has been damaged, deleted, or corrupted. It can be caused by a virus, a hard re-boot, a power outage or surge, disc-partitioning utilities; sometimes updating software, anti-virus programs, or simply installing new software can damage a partition.

- **Computer keeps re-booting.** The most common reason a computer keeps re-booting over and over is because the boot sector has been hijacked by a virus that creates a continuous loop. It keeps telling the system to go back to the boot sector and re-boot.

- **System freezes or hangs.** When your system freezes or hangs while trying to boot or while accessing a file or program, it usually indicates that there are bad sectors on the hard drive and the system is unable to access the information it needs to open the file or load the program. It can be caused by a corrupt file, shared program files that have conflicting call procedures, or too many system resources are being used (the system memory gets full or overloaded).

- **Drive or device not found.** When you get a message telling you the drive is not ready or that the hard drive or device is not found, it could mean the hard drive is bad, the boot priority in BIOS has been changed, the partition structure is damaged, or a virus has infected your system.

- **Operating system not found.** An "operating system not found" message typically means that the operating system files are damaged, the boot device priority has been changed, the partition table is damaged, or the hard drive has been formatted.[17]

What to Do in the Midst of a Crash

A sense of panic can quickly overtake us if we suspect our system is crashing. We might start hitting keys, moving our mouse furiously in an effort to get the system to respond, or pick up the phone to ask for help. While these are all natural responses, this is not the time to debate or search for help. If you suspect damage, act now and pick up the phone later. Time can be your friend or enemy depending upon how quickly you take action.

- **Listen carefully (but quickly).** Listen to your system and make a mental note of the sound. Is your computer making a clicking sound or does it sound more like grinding? These details do matter, so don't spend a lot of time listening, but be aware of the specific sound as you are reaching for the power button.

- **Turn off your computer.** This is not the time to experiment or hit specific keys to see what happens. The longer your system is on, the more potential for damage. Keep your ears open and your finger moving to the power button.

- **Write it down.** While the incident is still fresh in your mind, document exactly what happened. What did the screen look like? What was your first indication that something went wrong?

- **Find an expert (and choose wisely).** While many of us have friends or relatives who are technically savvy and knowledgeable, your hard drive and its contents should be handled by someone who deals with these issues for a living. You're likely to find someone local who can assist you in recovering your data, but if not, sending the system to a qualified and reputable expert is a small inconvenience for getting your precious pictures, banking information, and other items restored.

Is There a (Computer) Doctor in the House?

Fortunately, there are many highly qualified companies that can rescue your precious pictures and other critical information (such as banking information or confidential work files) if your system crashes. You will need to do a bit of homework to determine which company is the best choice for your needs. (See the "Resources" section for a more comprehensive listing).

Credentials in this arena are particularly important; you'll want to check their website for customer references, industry awards and endorsements, and other credibility-related information. Are they quoted in trusted magazines? While these things don't completely guarantee that the company will live up to its promises, they provide an extremely important filtering process. You can take some comfort in knowing this company has been evaluated by industry professionals and has stood up to real scrutiny. Anyone can open a data-recovery company these days; it is a multimillion-

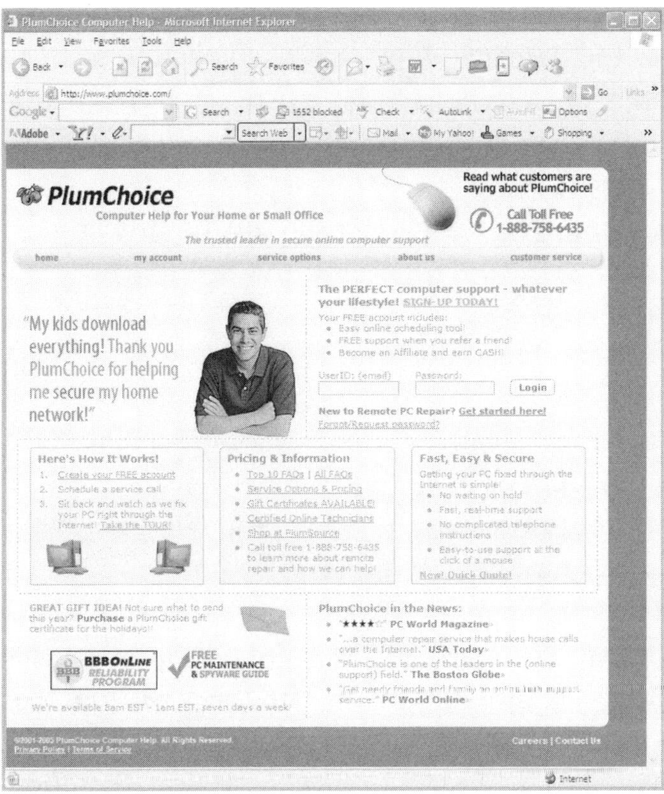

Photo 8A

Look no further than the Web for handholding when it comes to your computer-related issues. Companies such as PlumChoice provide online help that still connects you with a live person. *Image reproduced with permission from PlumChoice.*

dollar industry that attracts top industry professionals *and* less-than-honest operators. A little due diligence will go a long way.

Pricing may be a bit confusing at first. While the lowest price doesn't ensure a shoddy job, the highest quote doesn't ensure the best offering either.

To get a price quote for a data recovery service, you'll need to provide the following information regarding your system:

- Operating system (Windows XP, Windows 2000, and so on)
- The size of the damaged hard drive (40 GB, and so on)
- What happened right before the crash
- What you did (give as much detail as possible) when you realized it was crashing
- How much time you believe lapsed during this process
- What kinds of critical data are on the drive (financial, business, pictures, and so on)
- How quickly you need the data recovered

Some companies may charge you an evaluation fee. Make sure you understand what the charges cover and why it is warranted. Also, make sure to have your account information ready. You will likely need to have your product ID and key numbers, which can be found on the CPU itself (in the form of a sticker with a bar code) or on the bottom of a laptop.

Most data can be recovered in a few days, depending upon the damage and the company's current workload. They may be able to give you a time frame, but don't be too upset if they miss it by a day or so. They are involved in delicate work. Also, ask how they will communicate their progress. Will they notify you if they run into a particular problem right away? Will they call to let you know if a deadline or other key issue changes?

For those of you who have confidential banking data and other information on your computer, it is important to take extreme care with choosing the right company. Some companies specialize in handling confidential data and offer to sign a non-disclosure agreement regarding what they see on your computer. Customer references will be particularly important in this situation.

Trying a Data Recovery Program First

If you're a bit wary of spending the money to send your hard drive to a data recovery team, you may wish to try a software program, called a data recovery program, at home first. There are data recovery software programs and image recovery programs. One headache you will encounter is that in many cases, the original file name is lost, so you may have to rename and identify all of your photos or documents again. If an individual photo has been damaged, the recovery may result in an incomplete photo that might be saved by cropping or eliminating the corrupt area of the photo. Half the loaf is better than none.

Don't look for the least expensive software program on the market; in these instances, you may find you get exactly what you pay for. When your pictures are at risk, it is worth a bit of research time and money to make sure you're giving yourself the best possible shot at rescuing those pictures. That doesn't mean you won't get a great price on the product; it just means you should verify a few things before spending the money and purchasing the software.

First, check the company's website for awards or what industry associations say about their product. Magazines such as *PC Magazine* give annual awards for a number of software products, and they put these products through a rigorous testing procedure. CNet (www.cnet.com) is another popular site that not only rates the software but also offers download solutions, some are rated freeware and others are available at a reasonable cost.

Second, how does the software handle the recovery process? Shy away from any product that writes anything at all to your damaged hard drive. This procedure can cause additional damage; ask questions about how the software works, and don't be afraid to pin the company rep down if you don't understand the process. Those of us in the technology field sometimes get a little caught up in our own jargon and don't do a good enough job of explaining what is happening in a way that makes sense.

Digital Camera Card Crashes

Although digital camera cards are much smaller than your hard drive, they do have many similarities. After all, these memory cards are much like a removable hard drive — one that you can carry around, put into your camera, and then put into your computer to transfer files.

Digital camera cards can experience damage on the card itself or in the card reader. Digital camera cards are small and mobile and fall victim to all kinds of real life mishaps. People have dropped them in the sink or spilled soda on them; they get stepped on, crushed in the bottom of a bag, or left in direct sunlight to overheat. These cards can also be damaged due to software issues or other computer-related processes. Their internal operating program gives instructions to the media card on many things, including how to store information on the card itself. Sometimes the camera doesn't realize it has reached the maximum capacity of the card (like when you reach the last frame on a roll of 35mm film), and it may overwrite some important information at the beginning string on the card. Luckily, these little memory cards can often be rescued from accidents and carelessness.

Accidental Deletion

Sometimes things happen, and technology can be a testy partner, particularly at the most inopportune moments. Or, you may think that your spouse downloaded all the pictures onto the hard drive when he thought you had done the same, and before you know it, you just zapped all fifty pictures from your very first marathon. Fortunately, if you accidentally delete your digital pictures from your camera card, it is likely that you can recover them. You see, even though your camera tells you the card is empty, the images aren't really erased. As long as you don't write anything else over the card (meaning, taking more pictures), it is likely you can recover your photographs. When you delete a file from your media card, the actual file itself isn't deleted. There is a tag for that file in the file allocation table (FAT), and that space is registered as being available. Some equate the FAT to a table of contents for a hard drive — the table is just reorganized; the information is still there.

Thankfully, very few digital cameras "zero out" a media card when it is formatted. So, if you just deleted your pictures, take heart (but don't take any more pictures).

There are several software products on the market designed to help you recover deleted digital pictures. One of the most popular products is called PhotoRescue from a company called DataRescue, Inc. (www.datarescue.com). This software is available for both Mac and Windows operating systems and is compatible with almost every kind of digital media card. The company allows you to download a trial version of the software, and this product has demonstrated a high success rate among industry magazines and web resources. There are also a number of other programs from which to choose, and a web search will quickly yield numerous results for you to evaluate.

Memory Card Errors

I recently had an experience with a memory card error. Against my better judgment, I used my brand new digital camera and memory card to shoot pictures of my five-year-old daughter's birthday party. I kept my previous model digital camera in my pocket as a backup, but really should have used another (less important) event to break out my shiny new camera. Even those of us who know better don't always do what we're supposed to do. Fortunately, it was a repeatable error, and I was able to take the card back to my local photo store and exchange it for another one. The pictures survived, but I learned my lesson. This makes for great book and magazine material, but it's a painful way to get it. I worried about the pictures the entire day.

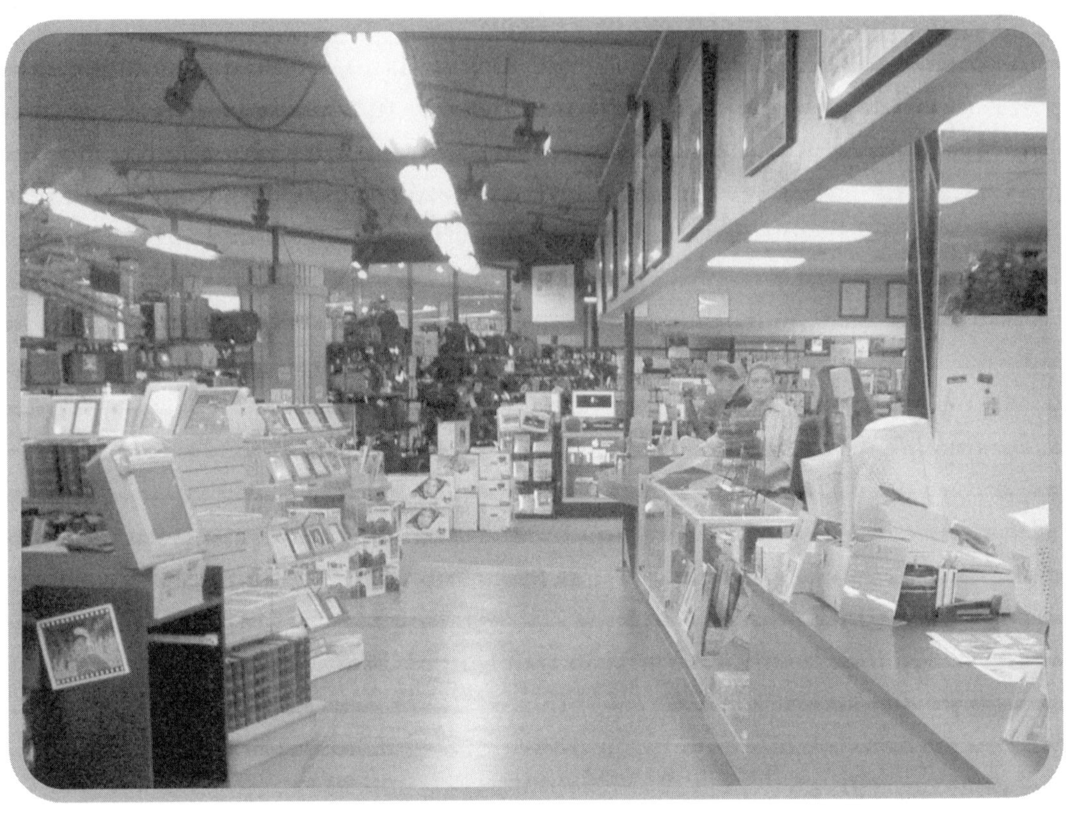

Photo 8B
Your trusted photo lab can also help you in a time of crisis. Call ahead to find out if they offer retrieval and recovery services.

If you get a card error displayed on your LCD screen, it's best to get the camera connected to your computer and immediately download the images if at all possible. Sometimes the error is due to incompatibility between the camera and a certain kind of card and sometimes it is due to the camera itself.

After downloading your pictures, if you find some or all of them missing, it's time to find an image-recovery program. Like those made for hard drive failures, there are several software programs available to help rescue images from digital camera cards. Some programs handle both memory card failures and hard drive failures. They are priced well and are often reviewed by today's top computer publications.

Also, don't forget your trusted photo lab in this situation! There are many photo stores and consumer electronics stores that will handle this recovery for you and can even walk you through preventive measures in the future. Call your local photo shop and ask if they offer these kinds of services.

The Big Picture

If you've ever experienced a hard drive failure, take heart that you are not alone. The majority of all computer users have experienced a hard drive crash and lost important information as a result. You have an advantage now. You not only understand that losing data is possible, you know how to handle it. You'll also be far more likely to perform the regular backup measures promoted in this book and will rest easier knowing your favorite photographs are better protected than they've ever been.

- If you care about the information, take the time to back up your images regularly. If you've come back from an important trip or event and have lots of photos, back them up as soon as you've transferred them to your hard drive. At the very least, strongly consider an external hard drive to mirror all of the data — including your directories and email files. Low-cost hard drive image software will allow you to capture all of the content on your hard drive so you can restore everything. In addition, make additional CD or DVD copies (two or three) of all of your irreplaceable photos, documents, and videos.

- Perform regular utilities on your hard drive such as Disk Clean Up and Disk Defragmenter (found under System Tools).

- If your digital camera gives you a low-battery warning, it's time to stop shooting. If your camera battery runs dry in the middle of saving a picture to the removable card, all of the pictures on the card could be damaged and the card rendered unreadable.

- Don't remove your media card until you're sure it is finished writing the picture to the hard drive. Some readers give you an option in the toolbar to "eject hardware" so that you can safely remove the card. Click on the "eject hardware" button in your toolbar to properly stop the process before removing the card.

- Most consumers give little thought to backup and disaster recovery. But with today's hefty-sized hard drives, it is impossible to stress strongly enough the importance of protecting your pictures. They represent important moments in your family and your life. They help you remember weddings, birthdays, special events, vacations, parents, and loved ones who are no longer with you. A second hard drive can be a life- and memory-saver. Two or three CD or DVD copies can be the added insurance you may be glad you took out in the protection of your photos.

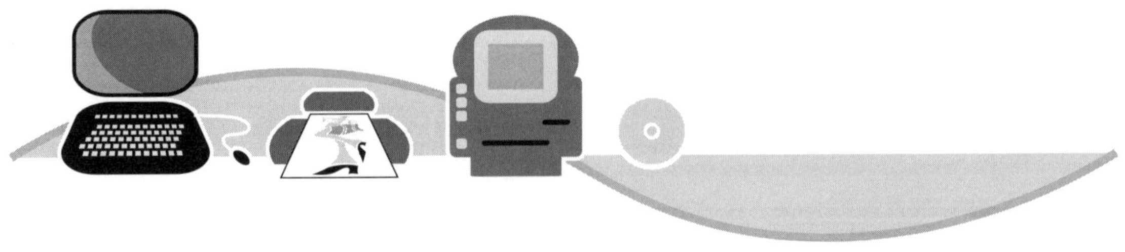

9

Ahead of the Curve

Keeping up with Changing Technology

Diane looked forward to spring cleaning with the same enthusiasm she reserved for visits to the dentist and her Ob-Gyn. It was a rite of passage for her, though, and she always enjoyed how light she felt after weeding through old boxes and taking still-useful-but-not-used-by-her items to her local thrift store.

There was just one box she never knew how to handle. Each year, she'd move the thing around to another place in the hopes it would take care of itself or somehow disappear without the commitment required of having to throw it out. She dreaded each time she happened upon the box, and yet, she couldn't get herself to do anything more than open the lid, rifle through the contents, and then close the box, tucking it away in a new location until she could repeat the process twelve months in the future.

Inside the box resided stacks of floppy disks and SyQuest disks. She had vague memories of what might be on those disks but had no way to read them. Floppy drives and SyQuest drives were harder to come by than a cure for the common cold. She remembered some early digital pictures and designs she'd created for clients and believed some of the work was worth resurrecting. Did she back up her business financial records on floppy disks back then? She couldn't remember.

"This is ridiculous," she huffed to herself as she considered her commitment issues might now extend to throwing out old computer disks. After all, if she couldn't read them, chances were that no one else could either. In a moment of bravado, she marched the entire box out to her dumpster, turned it upside down and watched the small avalanche of black, plastic rectangles mingle with old catalogs and plastic wrappers.

She peeked over her shoulder and second-guessed herself. What if there was something really important on those disks? She wondered what her neighbors would think of seeing her dumpster-diving in her own front yard.

Are you one of those people who have floppy disks you can't read? You keep them in your desk drawer and just maneuver around them as you search for a highlighter or some tape? Maybe you've also got old home movies or 35mm slides you can't readily read since locating equipment to read those formats can be as elusive as the single socks that continue escaping from the dryer. Sure, you could go online and hunt down one of these readers, maybe even find it on eBay, but then you'd have the joyful task of setting it up and reading every disk to determine whether the contents were worth saving or not. Sometimes not knowing is just easier.

Technology will continue to evolve and we will benefit in countless ways because of it, but those evolutions have costs too, and one of them is the real likelihood that we'll have important information on disks we can't access.

"I have over a hundred floppy disks I can't read,"[18] says Ted Werth, the founder of Plum Choice, a company that provides computer assistance via the Web. The fact that someone as tech-savvy as Werth has unreadable floppies speaks to the widespread nature of this problem. It's a combination of time, energy, and nuisance that make what industry insiders call "technology migration" a real problem for those of us who find our lives increasingly digital.

Those in the graphics industry may remember the company SyQuest with fondness and frustration. The once publicly-traded company made a line of popular removable media drives and disks and was heavily relied upon by many in the graphic arts industry. They were touted as a solid mobile media and were perfect for long-term storage as well. Many graphic designers, including Sarah Handlos, president of Postmarks Design in Austin, Texas, once used SyQuest disks for image transfer and storage. Now she has several disks in her office and no way to read them.

Unfortunately, SyQuest filed for bankruptcy in 1998, and the assets and technologies later sold to Iomega Corporation. The company's website urged consumers to (on their own) try to locate any dealers or distributors that still had stock of the SyQuest drives so that people could remove the

Snapshots

Think outside the Frame

Don't be afraid to experiment! The beauty of digital photography is that you can take lots of pictures at no cost to you. You will be amazed at how your artistry improves by taking some risks and trying different things. Step away from the standard head-on shot and try shooting from a new angle, through an open window, or from another unique position. This is a great opportunity to practice the rule of thirds.

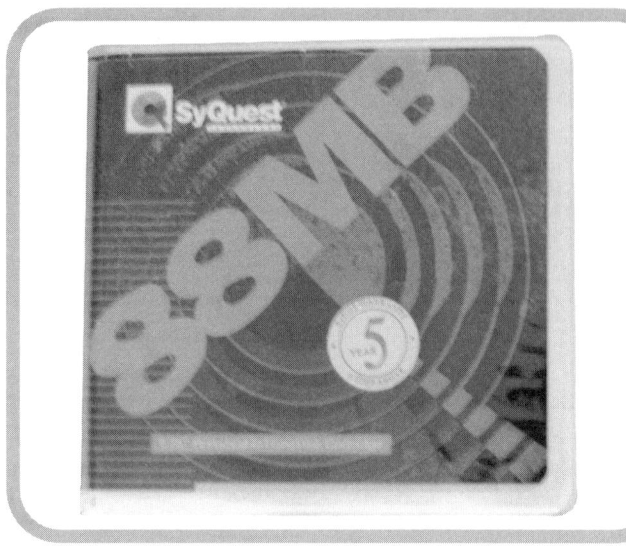

Photo 9A
Many people once stored all their images on SyQuest Disks and are now unable to access the images. Some experts predict that CDs will someday see a similar fate so we need to keep current on technology.

information from their disks. Of course, if the drives were to malfunction or stop working, that was a completely different problem.

This is a reality of the technology industry; some products will make it and others won't. Even those companies that seem invincible may find themselves vulnerable to evolving market demands, price wars, or changing consumer behavior.

"Each year in technology is equivalent to seventeen human years," states Werth. "People need to buy the latest technology whenever possible. Trying to save a few pennies now can mean substantial costs in the long run."[19]

Technology Migration 101

Technology migration simply refers to taking important files such as digital pictures, video, and financial documents and transferring them from one technology or format to another. Many companies deal with this issue when they move to a new computer platform, upgrade software, or even change telephone systems. Fortunately, we're in the position of dealing with migration issues on a much smaller and more manageable level.

There are two aspects of this issue to consider: hardware and software. Software refers to not only the types of operating systems and image-editing software programs we use, but it also (in this case) refers to the types of file formats used in digital photography. Some common picture file formats are JPEG, TIFF, and BMP.

Hardware refers to any equipment used for reading these files or running software. The most troublesome part of managing changes in technology involves hardware because there are so many companies manufacturing so many products, and oftentimes they use their own standards rather than adapting to industry uniformity. This is done in part to make their product different and to keep customers loyal to their line of products, but it can also lead us down a path of obsolete equipment with no way to access our pictures and important files in the future.

How to Keep Up

"At some point in the future, we will have at least one massive migration movement,"[20] says Werth, who recalls previous massive migrations of VHS to DVD, cassette to CD, and floppy to CD as but a few such transitions we've witnessed. Many believe that the current debate between the two DVD formats — Blu-Ray and HD-DVD — will be the next major transition we as consumers will make. These two technologies use different formats and are incompatible with current technology, so at some point you will need to decide which one will replace the DVD player you now use.

As someone who regularly reads industry trade information, reports, company press announcements, white papers, and journals, I can feel overwhelmed by the constant barrage of announcements and analysis of new products, standards, software, and research. Just keeping up with the

Snapshots

For the Kids — Background Check

We've all been there. We have a perfect shot, only to find we have a telephone pole that appears to be shooting out of someone's head. Keep your background simple and look for intruders such as cars, trash cans, or stray magazines. If shooting outside, consider a healthy sized tree as the background. Nature provides wonderful support for our favorite photographs.

changes for my own writing assignments requires a litany of Windows folders, email directories, outlines, and charts.

Because your life is probably a bit like juggling balls of butter while roller skating, we're going to look at this issue strictly from the perspective of making sure you can let a decade or two pass and still be able to access your pictures.

Do You Save Pictures on Media Cards?

In doing research for this book, I was surprised to find there is a small group of people who don't download their pictures from their memory card to their computer, but rather, fill up their memory cards and then buy more when the card is full. In fact, Werth states that one of his relatives used to fill up a media card, take it to her local photo shop for prints, and then purchase another media card. She used the card as a storage device as well as digital film. Fortunately, she had an expert in the family, and Werth helped her create a better system.

While some companies promote being able to store your images on a removable media card, this method of storage poses some potential problems. There is no easy way to label these cards, making the ability to easily recognize what pictures are on the card a challenge. We also need to remember that removable camera cards can be subject to technology changes, and you may find the format your camera uses gets phased out over time, leaving them to share storage space with your floppy disks and old home movies.

Keep up with Your Standards

"It's best to stay toward standardized media whenever possible,"[21] states Werth, who counsels that standard off-the-shelf technology has a greater chance of being read by newer products as they come into the market.

Werth's advice is in line with what many other industry experts advise. This doesn't mean that you shouldn't experiment with exciting new devices; it just means that when it comes to a long-term strategy for your digital pictures, make sure your pictures are written in a standard format and can be accessed digitally.

Snapshots

Did You Know?
Although color photography as we know it became popular in the 1950s, creating color photographs had been experimented with during the 1800s. The first permanent color picture was taken by James Clerk Maxwell in 1861.

The good news for digital photographers is that these cameras use industry-accepted file formats like JPEG, which many experts agree will continue to be readable indefinitely by future software programs because they are so universally adopted. Many of today's most popular software programs are "backward compatible," meaning they can read files from earlier versions of software. A simple text file that was written twenty years ago can still be read today.

Didn't You Say Not to Store Pictures on the Hard Drive?

Let me explain.

In archiving your pictures and protecting them in the future, it is important not to store them ONLY on your hard drive. Statistically, many of these drives will fail within their MTBF (mean time before failure) rate. However, at least one set should be kept on your hard drive, especially when migrating from an old computer to a new one.

Keeping files on a standardized media (computer hard drive) greatly increases your chances that you'll be able to access those pictures long after other hardware storage devices (floppy, SyQuest, and so on) have come and gone. The pictures are digital and easily accessed.

It seems that, when it comes to hard drives, we can't live with them and we can't live without them!

Tracking Trends: A Quick Course

This particular topic can be unruly at times because of the sheer volume of new product introductions that come out each year. For those interested in seeing what might be the next big platform, there are several sources you can check for insight. You can also test out a few things yourself, a strategy I find particularly valuable.

First and foremost, scan a few computer magazines or websites (check out appendix B). Many trade and consumer publications tend to follow similar issues and cover some of the same topics, so it won't be long before you are able to notice a trend or see that a new format is getting particular attention. You'll find yourself becoming knowledgeable of these issues in no time.

Second, take the time to visit an electronics store or two and play with some gadgets. For those who feel a little apprehensive, this can be a bit of a challenge, but there is nothing that will give you confidence faster than holding a product in your hands and asking someone to give you some information about it. Go to a retail store you like and keep talking to people until you find someone who can give you the answers you're looking for. If you aren't getting an answer in a way that makes sense to you, don't fear asking a stupid question. There are no stupid questions. Sometimes those in technology have a little trouble translating their industry jargon into a common sense explanation, and trust me, by requiring this of your acronym-loving sales rep, you're doing him a favor. Confused people never buy.

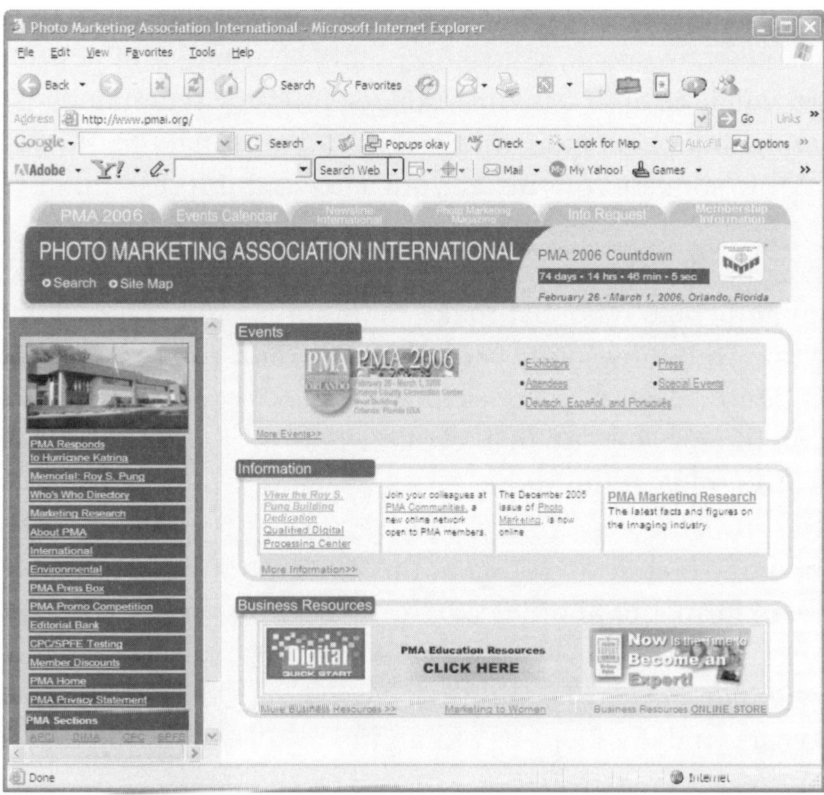

Photo 9C
Photo industry organizations, such as the well-regarded Photo Marketing Association, provides numerous resources to the public and can help you keep current of new announcements and industry trends. Image reproduced with permission from the Photo Marketing Association.

The Big Picture

Consider the exploration of emerging technologies one that might open new doors of interest to you. Learning about changing technology is actually a pretty interesting topic. Once you get familiar with some of the acronyms and geek speak, your comprehension rate will continue to escalate, and you'll be able to better understand new technology issues and how they might impact your professional and personal life. If nothing else, you can throw some acronyms at your kids and impress them with your prowess.

Tech people like acronyms. Some of us in the industry are convinced that there are people who just make them up for fun. They don't have to mean anything but they sound cool. The next time you're trapped at a company function or dinner party, you can open up a discussion by asking opinions on the Blu-Ray/HD-DVD format wars.

I know. I should get out more.

- Technology migration refers to the movement from one hardware or software format to another.

- We will likely see at least one major migration issue in the next several years, and it will affect our ability to access our digital pictures in the future.

- Today's top line of digital cameras write files in standard formats such as JPEG, and this will help greatly in being able to read your digital pictures for years to come.

- When looking at how to store digital pictures, consider using a standard technology such as a CD and a standard file such as JPEG; industry standards are usually easier to migrate to a new technology when it comes out and are considered by manufacturers when designing new products.

- Read a few computer or digital photography magazines to keep an eye on possible trends. Scan some top computer and photo websites for updated information on formats and new issues related to digital photography.

- When it's time for you to upgrade your computer, it's also a great time to learn about which new technologies will assist you in keeping your digital photographs readable. You'll already be in a learning mode and can incorporate questions about your current backup methods and file formats into your shopping experience, streamlining the entire process.

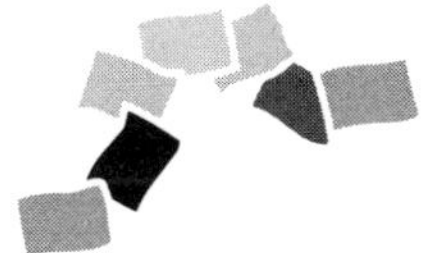

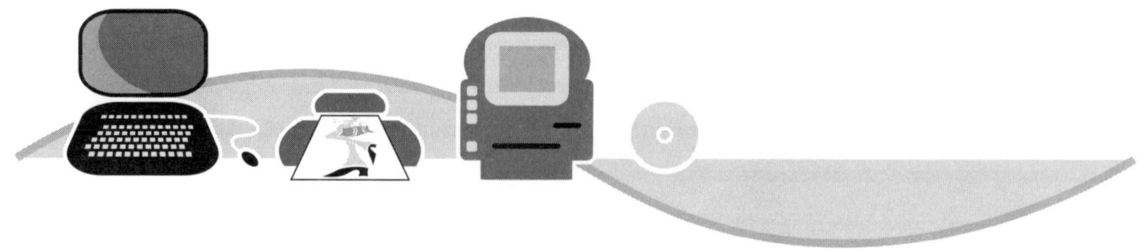

Afterword

So, how do you make the time for this? This is the million-dollar question, isn't it?

Without getting too philosophical, each of us has to decide what is most important in our lives, and it is real work each day trying to fit in those things we know are most important to us. If you're like many people, you'd do just about anything to make sure your favorite photographs are around for loved ones and future generations to enjoy. Much of what your children, grandchildren, and relatives will know about your family, your time on Earth, and your lineage will be a direct result of the actions you take today.

Yet the everyday process of preserving those photographs ranks right up there with regular physicals, dental work, and rotating our tires. The things we know are most important are also the things that we tend to neglect until a crisis occurs.

That said, if you're looking for a regular schedule to follow or some semblance of a plan, consider doing your homework when you're getting ready to upgrade your home or home office computer. You'll already be in the mode of sorting through old files, and you'll be shopping and comparing the latest features, technologies, and compatibility issues. This is a great time to better understand what technologies might be obsolete and which ones may stand the test of time. This is also a great time to verify your archive files are still readable. If they're on a format that is in jeopardy, use this transition to move your images to another backup method.

To some extent, technology will always be a bit of an unwieldy beast to manage. That is part of the complexity of progress; it will introduce new benefits and new chaos into our lives, and we will have to decide which issues deserve our attention.

When I think of my own children, I desperately want them to be able to relive their childhood through our family photo library for decades to come. They all love to look at their photos on the computer screen or on the refrigerator, and these images excite them and encourage conversations that help us relive those events. They are moments of joy revisited.

It is this thought that keeps me focused on making sure our legacy is protected.

Well, this thought and guilt. Guilt always works on us moms.

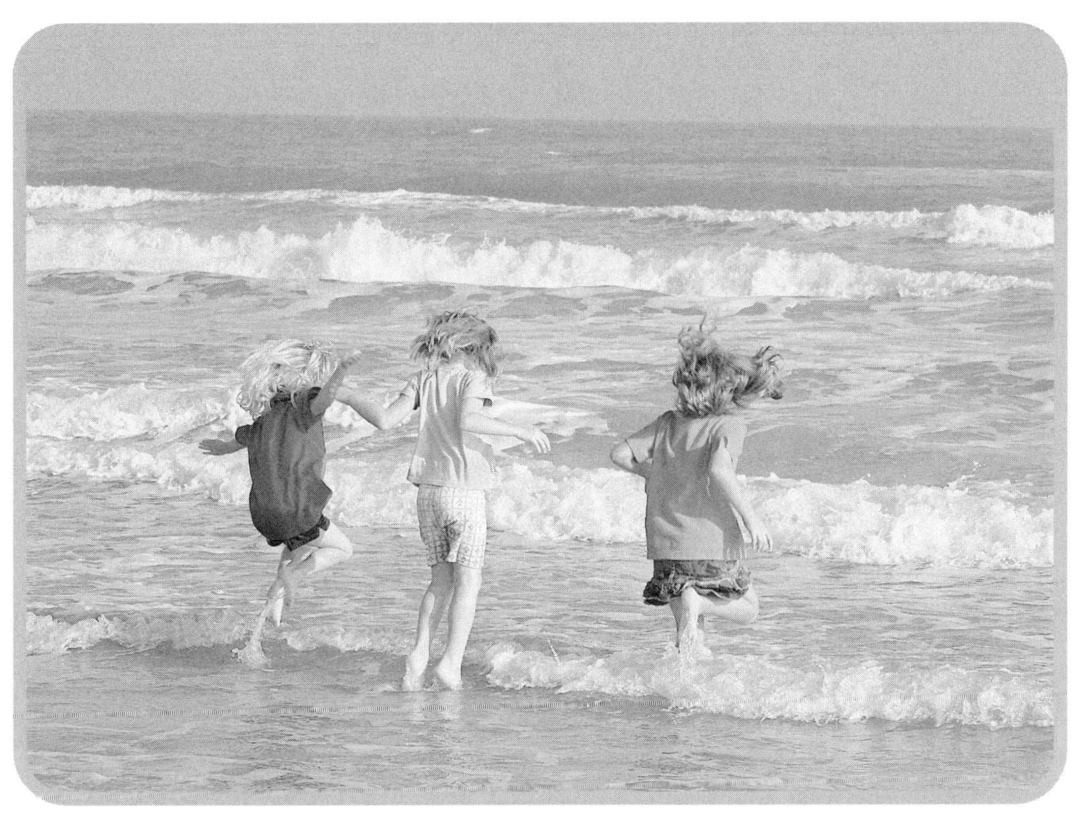

The moment may be fleeting, but the memories will remain.
Share your stories.
Protect your pictures.
Leave a legacy.

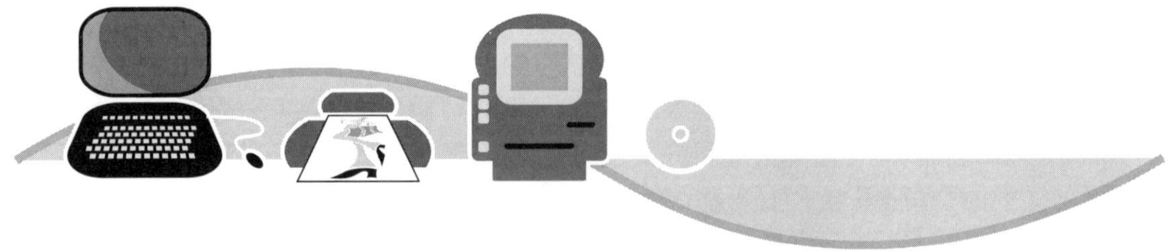

Appendix A

Quick Reference Guide

Want to know how many digital pictures will fit on your camera card? Here is a guide containing the latest information. It has been provided courtesy of crucial.com. No more fretting about when you're going to run out of space on the card!

With a 2-megapixel camera	
Card size	*Number of photos*
128mb	122
256 mb	244
512mb	523
1gb	1,046

With a 4-megapixel camera	
Card size	*Number of photos*
128mb	61
256 mb	122
512mb	244
1gb	512

With a 3-megapixel camera	
Card size	*Number of photos*
128mb	76
256 mb	154
512mb	327
1gb	655

With a 5-megapixel camera	
Card size	*Number of photos*
128mb	49
256 mb	99
512mb	209
1gb	409

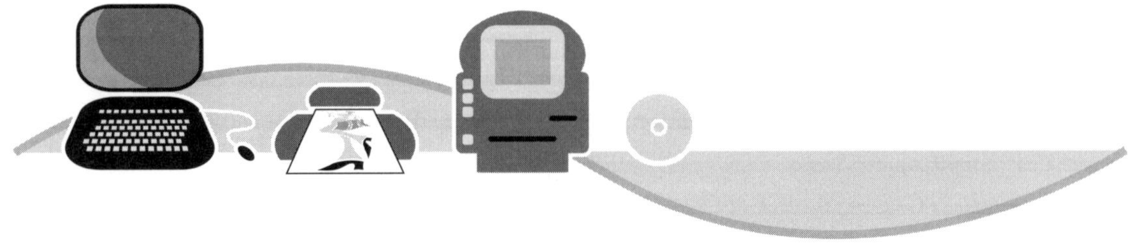

Appendix B

Resources

Education and Information Resources

Better Photo™
(offers courses, workshops, articles, forums, and other great resources)
Jim Moitke, Founder
PO Box 2781
Redmond, WA 98073
www.betterphoto.com

CNET (c/net)
www.cnet.com

The CD-Info Company
Katherine Cochrane, Founder and President
1697 Willard Rd., NW
Palm Bay, FL 32907-6320
321-432-9703
www.cd-info.com

Digital Photography Review™
www.dpreview.com

DIY Network (Do It Yourself)
ww.diynetwork.com

How Stuff Works
www.howstuffworks.com

Kim Komando
Nationally syndicated radio host offering a plethora of information on the radio and online, including newsletters and books

WestStar TalkRadio Network
The WestStar Building
2711 N. 24th Street
Phoenix, AZ 85008-1044
602-381-8200
www.komando.com

Marken Communications
Industry communications company with resources online regarding storage, backup, and recovery
3375 Scott Blvd #108
Santa Clara, CA 95054-3113
(408) 986-0100
www.markencom.com

Pictures Matter
3100 Meridian Park, N-265
Greenwood, IN 46142
317-422-5199
www.picturesmatter.com

ShortCourses
Dennis P. Curtin
www.shortcourses.com

Wilhelm Imaging Research (Print Permanence Expert)
www.wilhelm-research.com

Consumer Electronics and Digital Photography Magazines

Digital Camera
4045 Sunset Lane, Ste A
Shingle Springs, CA 95682
www.digicamera.com

Digital Photographic
Highbury Entertainment Ltd.,
Paragon House
St. Peters Road, Bournemouth,
Dorset BH1 2JS UK
44 (0) 1202 299900
www.paragon.co.uk

Digital Photo Pro
Werner Publishing Offices
12121 Wilshire Blvd., Suite 1200
Los Angeles, CA 90025-1176
310-820-1500

PC Magazine
28 East 28th St.
New York, NY 10016-7930
212-503-3500
www.pcmag.com

Photo Marketing *Magazine*
3000 Picture Place
Jackson, MI 49201
517-788-8100
www.photomarketing.com

Photo Industry Reporter
7600 Jericho Tpke.
Woodbury, NY 11797
516-364-0016
photoreporter@att.net
www.photoreporter.com

Imaging Business *Magazine*
Cygnus Business Media
3 Huntington Quadrangle
Suite 301N
Melville, NY 11747
631-845-2700
www.labsonline.com
www.imaginginfo.com

Picture Business *Magazine*
1500 Spring Garden Street
Ste. 1200
Philadelphia, PA 19130
215-238-5300
Fax: 215-238-5457
www.picturebusinessmag.com

Photo Trade News
Cygnus Business Media
3 Huntington Quadrangle
Suite 301N
Melville, NY 11747
631-845-2700
www.imaginginfo.com

PHOTOgraphic *Magazine*
6420 Wilshire Blvd.
Los Angeles, CA 90048
323-782-3600
www.photographic.com

Rangefinder *Magazine*
PO Box 1703
1312 Lincoln Boulevard
Santa Monica, CA 90406
310-451-8506
www.rangefindermag.com

Shutterbug *Magazine*
1419 Chaffee Drive, Suite 1
Titusville, FL 32780
321-269-3212
www.shutterbug.com

Wired *Magazine*
660 3rd Street, 1st Floor
San Francisco, CA 94107
415-276-8400
Fax: 415-276-8500
www.wired.com

Photography Books

Digital Photography All-in-One Desk Reference for Dummies
by David D. Busch
ISBN 0764573284

Digital Photography for Dummies, Fifth Edition
by Julie Adair King
ISBN 0764598023

Going Visual: Using Images to Enhance Productivity, Decision Making, and Profits
by Alexis Gerard and Bob Goldstein
www.goingvisual.com
ISBN 041710253

PC Magazine Guide to Digital Photography
by Daniel Grotta and Sally Weiner Grotta and John Wiley & Sons (Oct. 2004) ISBN 0764573721
Related Author Websites:
www.wellconnectedwoman.com and www.digitalbenchmarks.com

PC Magazine Guide to Printing Great Digital Photos
by David Karlins
John Wiley & Sons (Sept. 2004)
ISBN 0764575783

The BetterPhoto Guide to Digital Photography
by Jim Miotke
PO Box 2781
Redmond, WA 98073
Order at www.betterphoto.com

The Savvy Guide to Digital Photography
by Paula M. Kalamaras and Paul T. Kraly
Indy-Tech Publishing (May 2005)
ISBN 0790613043

Step-by-Step Digital Photography: A Guide for Beginners
by Jack Drafahl and Sue Drafahl
Amherst Media (Sept. 2004)
ISBN 1584281413

Online Photo Service Companies

Kodak EasyShare Gallery
Kodak Imaging Network
1480 64th St., Suite 300
Emeryville, CA 94608
510-229-1200
www.kodakgallery.com

PhotoWorks®
Seattle, Washington
www.photoworks.com

Shutterfly
2800 Bridge Parkway, Suite 101
Redwood City, CA 94065
650-610-5200
Fax: 650-654-1299
www.shutterfly.com

Snapfish
303 Second Street
South Tower, Suite 500
San Francisco, CA 94107
415-979-3700
415-979-3708
www.snapfish.com

SmugMug
www.smugmug.com

LifePics
5777 Central Avenue, Suite 120
Boulder, CO 80301
(303) 413-9500
www.lifepics.com

Winkflash
112b Dillabur Avenue
North Kingstown, RI 02852
www.winkflash.com

Photo Editing Programs and Sharing Programs

Acdsee™8 Photo Manager

ACD Systems International, Inc.
PO Box 36
Saanichton, British Columbia
V8M 2C3 CANADA
250-544-6700
Fax: 250-544-0291
www.acdsee.com
www.acdsystems.com

Adobe Photoshop®

Adobe Systems, Inc.
345 Park Avenue
San Jose, CA 95110-2704
408-536-6000
www.adobe.com

Corel Photo Album 6 and Corel Paint Shop Pro X

Corel Corporation
1600 Carling Avenue
Ottawa, Ontario K1Z 8RZ
CANADA
www.corel.com

Hello (from Picasa)

www.hello.com

Photo Finale®

Trevoli, Ltd.
Dallas, Texas
www.photofinale.com

Picasa (from Google)

www.picasa.com

PiXPO

How2Share Technologies
Box 43028
Victoria, BC V8X 3G2
CANADA
www.pixpo.com

Hard Drive Backup and Recovery Resources

American Data Recovery

Many centers located throughout the country
800-450-9282
www.adrdatarecovery.com

DriveSavers Data Recovery

400 Bel Marin Keys Boulevard
Novato, CA 94949
800-440-1904
Fax: 415-883-0780
www.drivesavers.com

Data Recovery Services
2636 Walnut Hill Lane, Suite 230
Dallas, TX 75229
877-304-7189
After Hours Emergency:
214-924-6291
Fax: 214-350-8951
www.datarecovery.net

NovaBACKUP 7.2
NovaStor Corporation
80B West Cochran
Simi Valley, CA 93065
805-579-6700
www.novastor.com

NTI NewTech Infosystems
NTI Backup NOW! 4.0 software
5 Mason, Suite 150
Irvine, CA 92618-2552
949-421-0720
info@ntius.com
www.ntius.com

PhotoRescue and DataRescue
40 Bld iercot
4000 Liege (Belgium)
32-4-3446510
www.datarescue.com

Plum Choice
Computer help over the Internet
143 The Great Road, Suite 102
Bedford, MA 01730
888-758-6435
www.plumchoice.com

Xdrive
Xdrive, Inc.
1630 Stewart Street, Suite 140
Santa Monica, CA 90404
www.xdrive.com

Scrapbooking Resources and Specialty Resources

10•20•30 Minute Scrapbook Pages (Memories in the Making Scrapbooking)
by Nancy M. Hill, Candice Snyder, Rafael Nielson, Maren Ogden, Tarri Botwinski, Sharon Staples, and Julianne Smoot

Collected Memories
4633 Cass Street
San Diego, CA 92109
866-483-9391
www.collectedmemories.com

Creating Keepsakes Magazine
14850 Pony Express Road
Bluffdale, UT 84065
801-984-2070
www.creatingkeepsakes.com

Exposures®
1 Memory Lane
PO Box 3615
Oshkosh, WI 54903-3615
800-222-4947
800-699-6993 (fax)
www.exposuresonline.com

Legacy *Magazine*
22992 Mill Creek, Suite B
Laguna Hills, CA 92653
877-STAMPER
Fax: 949-380-9355
www.stampington.com

Memory Makers *Magazine*
12365 Huron Street, Suite 500
Denver, CO 80234-3438
800-366-6465
386-246-3404
www.memorymakersmagazine.com

Oriental Trading Company, Inc.
800-875-8480
www.orientaltrading.com

Quick & Easy Scrapbook Pages: 100 Scrapbook Pages You Can Make in One Hour or Less
by Memory Makers
ISBN 1892127202

Scrapbook.com Resources
www.scrapbook.com

Scrapbooking for Dummies
by Jeanne Wines-Reed and Joan Wines
ISBN 0764572083

Scrapbooks Etc.
PO Box 37789
Boone, IA 50037-0789
www.bhgscrapbooks.com

Photo Industry Associations

Consumer Electronics Association

2500 Wilson Blvd.
Arlington, VA 22201-3834
866-858-1555 or 703-907-7600
Fax: 703-907-7675
ce@ce.org
www.ce.org

I3A

701 Westchester Avenue
Suite 317W
White Plains, NY 10604
914-285-4937
www.i3a.org

Photo Marketing Association

3000 Picture Place
Jackson, MI 49201
517-788-8100
www.pmai.org

National Scrapbook Association

5127 Grand Phillips
Katy, TX 77450
713-589-2140
Fax: 713-589-2251
www.nsa.gs

Print on Demand

9439 Avenida Acero
Spring Valley, CA 91977
619-434-2165
Fax: 619-434-2165
www.printondemand.com

Industry Analysts (For Statistics and Market Trends)

IDC

5 Speen Street
Framingham, MA 01701
508-872-8200
www.idc.com

InfoTrends/CAP Ventures

97 Libbey Industrial Parkway
Suite 300
Weymouth, MA 02819
781-616-2100
Fax: 781-616-2121
info@infotrends-rgi.com
www.infotrends-rgi.com

Lyra Research, Inc.

320 Nevada Street, 1st Floor
PO Box 9143
Newtonville, MA 02460-9143
www.lyra.com

Future Image, Inc.
520 South El Camino Real, Suite 206A
San Mateo, CA 94402
650-579-0493
Fax: 650-579-0566
www.futureimage.com

Jonrel Imaging Consultants
70 Southwick Court
Rochester, NY 14623
585-292-1690
Fax: 585-292-6753
www.jonrel.com

NPD
900 West Shore Road
Port Washington, NY 11050
516-625-0700
www.npd.com

Photo Imaging News
10915 Bonita Beach Rd., Suite 1091
Bonita Springs, FL 34135
239-992-4421
Fax: 239-992-6328
www.photo-news.com

Photo Marketing Association
3000 Picture Place
Jackson, MI 49201
517-788-8100
www.pmai.org
www.photomarketing.com

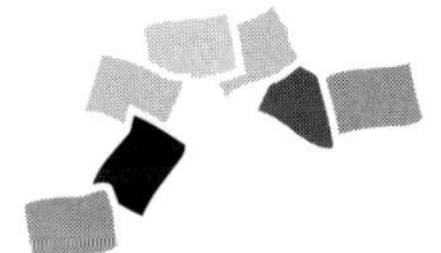

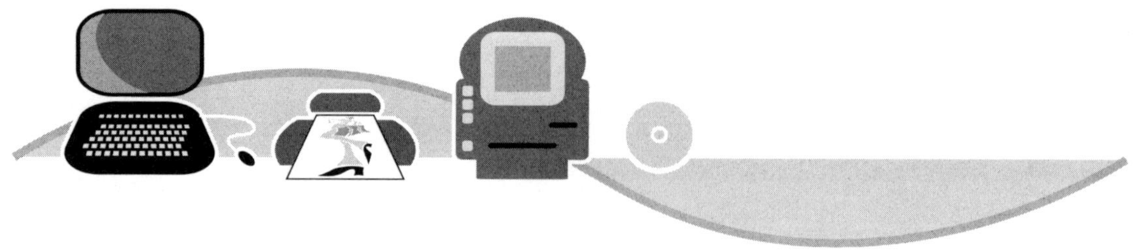

Appendix C

The FRAME Method™ Quick Reference Guide and Checklist

Here is a useful checklist to help you implement the FRAME Method™. For ease of use, it can also be downloaded from www.gotdigitalpictures.com.

Step 1: Filter Your Pictures

- ❑ Delete duplicate photos, poor shots, or unimportant pictures from hard drive
- ❑ Delete duplicate photos, poor shots, or unimportant pictures from camera card
- ❑ Delete duplicate photos, poor shots, or unimportant pictures from camera phone, PDA, or other portable device

- ❑ Get images in central location (computer hard drive)

Step 2: Reorganize by Marking Your Favorites

- ❑ Decide whether to use an image management program or the existing Windows folders.

  If using folders:

  - ❍ Decide how to segment your pictures (by month, year, season, or event)
  - ❍ Create file folders with appropriate names to begin organizing

  If using an image management program:

  - ❍ Consider features such as archiving CD features, marking favorites, and other sorting/enhancing tools
  - ❍ Play with trial versions first by downloading them from a website to see if you find the program easy to use
  - ❍ Check company's references, history, and awards won for their applications
  - ❍ Spend time playing and learning more about the features in your new image management program

- ❑ Make sure camera phone pictures and favorites emailed by loved ones have been saved on your hard drive and organized

- [ ] Go through pictures and mark your favorites for easy retrieval

Step 3: Archive Pictures Two Times with Two Methods in Two Locations

- [ ] Determine which methods you'd like to use (CD, DVD, online storage, external drive)

    - Consider CD if you would like to "spread the risk" by putting pictures on several CDs or would like to archive them by year or by event

    - Consider DVD if you'd like to fit the most pictures possible on one disk and streamline the archiving process (to save time), but remember they must be handled very carefully to avoid damage

- [ ] Back up all images to CD or DVD using image management program or CD-burning application

- [ ] Protect CDs /DVDs by storing them in jewel cases or specialty albums that offer archival properties and use intercept plastic

- [ ] Store CDs /DVDs in a secure location such as a fire safe or a safety deposit box

- [ ] Research online photo processing/storage companies to choose the best one that meets your needs (long-term storage, sharing, archiving services, and specialty products like photo books)

  - ❍ Check the "about us" section to verify reputation and history of service

- ❑ Consider external hard drive or other specialty backup device to help back up all your computer files on a regular basis

Step 4: Make a Print Using Archival Materials

- ❑ Make sure to use the manufacturer's suggested inks and paper for your home digital printer to give photos the best chance at long-term survival

- ❑ Consider using your online service to order copies of your favorite images, take your CDs or DVDs to your trusted photo retailer for prints, or upload them from home and pick them up at the store if they offer this service

- ❑ Store pictures in an archival box or in a specialty album using acid-free materials

Step 5: Ensure Backups Are Safe with an Annual Checkup

- ❑ Open CDs and DVDs to make sure you can still access the files

- ❑ Verify your disks are being properly stored (don't leave them out on top of your computer to collect dust)

- ❑ Check in with your online service provider to verify your account information is current (home address, phone, and email) and that there aren't any policy changes

- ❑ Open stored photo albums and scrapbooks and check the quality of your printed pictures

- ❑ Add current year's images to your backup system

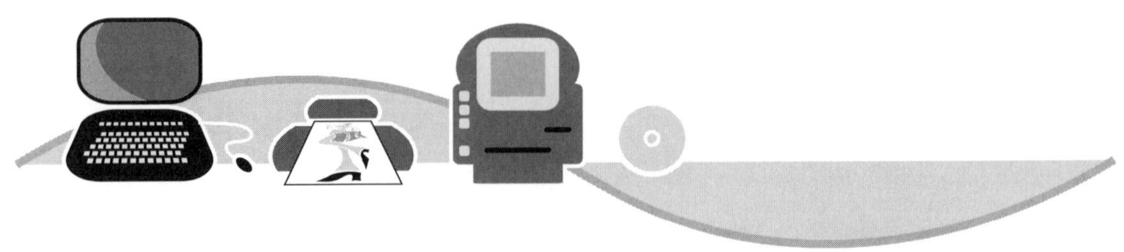

Endnotes

1. Eric Taub, "E.R. for Hard Drives," *The New York Times*, July 14, 2005.

2. Ibid.

3. Henry Wilhelm (co-founder, president, and director of research at Wilhelm Imaging Research, Inc.) in an interview with John Larish, summer 2005.

4. Peter Krogh (professional photographer and board member of American Society of Media Photographers), in discussion with the author, summer 2005.

5. Andy Marken (president of Marken Communications, Inc.), in discussion with the author, summer 2005.

6. Lisa Walker (president of I3A), in press release, December 15, 2004.

7. Andy Marken, summer 2005.

8. Ibid.

9. Mitch Goldstone in *Picture Business*. "Imaging Industry to Consumers: Print Those Image Files!" May 2005.

10. Kristy Holch (group director of InfoTrends/CAP Ventures), in discussion with the author, summer 2005.

11. Ibid.

12. Ibid.

13. Ibid.

14. Northern States Conservation Center, http://www.collectioncare.org (accessed summer 2005).

15. Henry Wilhelm, interview by Jefferson Graham, *USA Today*, February 17, 2005.

16. Alan Reiter (president of Wireless Internet & Mobile Computing, Inc.), in discussion with the author, summer 2005.

17. Courtesy of American Data Recovery, in discussion with the author, summer 2005.

18. Ted Werth (founder and president of Plum Choice), in discussion with the author, summer 2005.

19. Ibid.

20. Ibid.

21. Ibid.

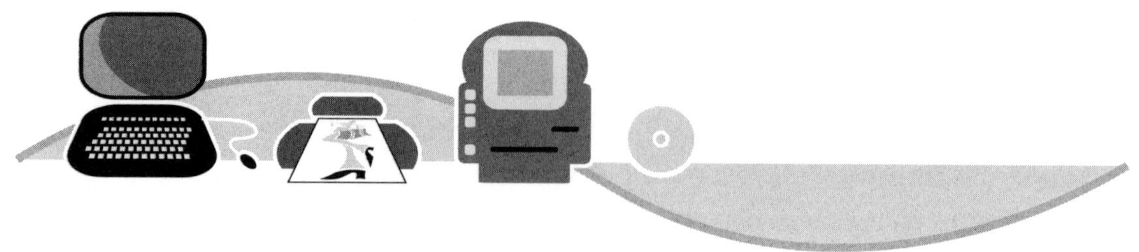

Glossary

acid free: Acid free products such as album pages, dividers, tissues, storage boxes, and mounting boards are designed to protect printed photographs to provide the most archival protection possible.

adapter: A piece of equipment that allows you to insert a smaller media card or other storage device into your computer. Because digital cameras use different media card formats, an adapter is often needed for the computer to read the device.

aperture: Light passes through the iris in the lens to expose film. The numbers can be a bit confusing at times, but the higher the number, the less amount of light hits the film (the numbering and light have an inverse relationship).

archival: Something that is considered to have good aging properties or will stand the test of time. The specific parameters of archival depend upon the issue, situation, and context.

aspect ratio: Determined by figuring the height and width of an image.

bit: Bit stands for *binary digit* and is the basic unit in the computer binary system. A one-bit system provides only black or white, and a single bit is either "on" or "off." More bits provide greater image depth.

bleed: A printing term that means that an image or colored (inked) area extends past or falls off a printed page. The bleed is the section that would run past margins or trim marks. The bleed is often helpful in correcting any misalignment so that color or an image covers all areas designated on the page.

byte: One byte equals 8 bits of digital information. A byte is a standard unit used to measure file size such as kilobytes (KB), megabytes (MB), gigabytes (GB), and terabytes (TB). See appendix A for how these are calculated in relation to megapixels in a digital camera.

C-41: This is the chemical processing system used for color negative film. Photo shops, drugstores, and other photo service stores use C-41 chemistry and equipment to process color film.

compression: A method of fitting more data into less space. Digital pictures are often compressed so that more pictures can be fit onto a memory card or more easily sent across the Internet.

contact sheet: A reference sheet that shows all images on a roll of film (or CD) so that you can easily tell which pictures are on which storage medium. Most photo processing stores offer contact sheets for digital pictures as well as for film processing.

crop: The way an image is trimmed or focused. For example, a picture showing someone's ex-wife (or ex-husband) can be cropped so that the former family member is no longer in the picture (literally and figuratively!). Crop is also a term used by scrapbookers for their art; they are often referred to as croppers and have cropping events or parties.

crop ratio: The height and width of a picture, such as 3 ½ x 5, 4 x 6, 5 x 7 and 8 x 10 (most commonly measured in inches). Sometimes, if you crop a picture, you'll need to select the right crop ratio for printing so that you don't accidentally cut off someone's head or other appendage!

CYMK: This acronym refers to cyan (C), magenta (M), yellow (Y), and black (K), which are the four printer colors mixed and used to create color pictures and graphics on ink-jet, laser, dye sublimation, and other press equipment. Many files being printed must be converted using software from RGB (red, green, blue) to CYMK, and color shifts do take place in this process.

densitometer: A specialized piece of equipment designed to measure the amount of light being reflected from a sample or picture. It is often used to verify accurate color ranges.

depth of field: How a picture's subject is focused in relation to the space in front of and behind the subject. For example, if your subject is far away, the depth of field will be larger than if your subject was close by. Different lenses, such as a wide-angle or telephoto, can increase your depth of field.

digital zoom: Often referred to as a *false zoom*, because the picture is magnified simply by enlarging the image without any extra details or pixels being added.

docking station: A device used by digital cameras that allows the camera to connect to a computer or a printer, making it easier to access the information (depending on the model) by simply slipping the camera into the dock for the images to be read or transferred. Some docks are designed to bypass computers completely and go straight to printers.

DPI: Stands for *dots per inch*. Imaging equipment such as scanners and printers are measured by DPI. The dot is the smallest unit that can be printed or scanned. The higher the DPI, the more detail that can be seen in the image. The higher the DPI, the larger the file, which means longer times in scanning, image processing, and printing.

dye sublimation: Dye sublimation is a continuous-tone printer that uses a thermal (heated) heat that vaporizes, or sublimates, the dye from a roll of color ribbon onto the specific dye-sublimation paper. Dye-sublimation printers are often used in digital photo kiosks and other retail printing methods. There are also lines of consumer printers that use a dye-sublimation process. These printers can also be used for creating specialty products (t-shirts, mugs, and so on) due to their heat-transfer design.

EXIF: The acronym stands for *exchangeable image file*, which is the file format that is used by many digital cameras. If a digital camera records a JPEG file, it is really recording and EXIF file and applying JPEG compression to shrink the picture's information to fit inside the EXIF file.

exposure: The letting in of light on a light-sensitive material. In digital camera terms, it is the amount of light that passes through a lens to form a picture.

f-stop: This is a specific numerical method that determines the size of the camera's lens opening. The higher the number, the less light is coming through the lens. This number is created by dividing the focal length of the lens by the aperture. So, f/8 lets in half the amount of light that f/4 allows.

flash media: Also called flash memory. This is a memory chip that can hold image information even after the equipment (such as a digital camera) has been shut off. This is helpful particularly if your digital camera's batteries die (if the unit is turned off — having them die while shooting can corrupt the media card).

gamma: If you change the gamma of an image, you are adjusting the brightness values of the middle tones of the picture.

histogram: Many software programs offer histograms, which are charts that show the values of the darkest and lightest areas of an image. A well-exposed image will show a graph that looks like a bell curve. If an image is underexposed (dark), it will be heavily weighted to the left hand side. If the image is overexposed (too light or blown out), it will be heavily weighted to the right hand side.

ink-jet: A method of printing that sprays ionized ink onto paper. Ink-jet printers continue to grow in popularity for printing pictures at home and are increasingly used for printing digital photographs.

interpolation: A method of increasing or decreasingly the number of pixels in a digital picture. Interpolation is used to make digital pictures larger by having a software program "copying" pixels nearby to "guess" what the image should contain. Interpolation is often used in conjunction with digital zoom and upsampling.

JPEG: The most commonly used digital picture file format. JPEG stands for *Joint Photography Experts Group*, the association that created the file format.

jump drive: Also called a USB drive or a flash drive, the jump drive is a flash memory storage device that can be plugged into a USB port and easily recognized by your computer. These drives are often used for backups or for transferring key files between computers (such as those who work from home and in the field or another office).

lag time: Also called shutter lag, this is the one thing that drives most digital camera users crazy. The lag time is the time between actually pressing the shutter release (button) to the camera actually taking the shot. In this time frame, subjects can move, causing blurred pictures and frustration. Digital camera manufacturers are increasingly improving shutter lag time.

LCD: LCD stands for *liquid crystal display*, which is a type of display used in digital cameras, portable computers, and other devices.

lossless compression: A method that makes sure that digital pictures experience no loss of quality because the uncompressed image is mathematically identical to the original; the image does not contain "made up" or interpolated pixels that can degrade an image's quality over time.

lossy compression: JPEG, for example, uses lossy compression, which means that certain aspects of a digital image are "invented" or interpolated as the picture is opened and closed. With each save, the image can degrade, causing loss of sharpness and other artifacts to surface in the picture. It helps to use the least amount of compression available on your digital camera; the images will be larger but they will remain in a higher quality state.

media card: Also called a memory card, which is the device that holds your digital pictures to be transferred to your computer, photo kiosk, online service, or printer.

megapixel: A megapixel is equal to one million pixels or larger. Cameras that have more megapixels (such as 3 megapixels and higher) create higher quality images than those lower range (often called "toy" cameras), but megapixel capability is not the only measure of making sure a digicam takes a quality picture. Lens design, optics, and other issues all play a factor in creating a high-quality digital image.

noise: Those little stray "artifacts" that can show up over time on a digital picture when it has been compressed a number of times. These stray pieces of information can indicate a picture has been compressed too often and should be protected through other means (such as printing).

Metadata: The data about the information or what is known about the file so that the picture can be accessed. For example, metadata may contain security information, manufacturer information, or other specialty content used by specific programs or hardware.

offline storage: Information that cannot be accessed from a computer or terminal until it is formatted or put into a specific drive to make it accessible.

online storage: Information that is stored in a way that can be accessed via the Internet. Many companies offer storage services based upon the size of the files and how long they are stored (photos, music, and video).

optical zoom: Optical zooms are much preferred to digital zooms because optical zooms will focus in on an image without falsely creating parts of the picture. Optical zoom is considered "true focus," meaning that the image will remain the same quality but just encompassing a smaller frame of a scene. When purchasing a digital camera, look for the optical zoom figure.

PictBridge: An industry technology that allows you to transfer images directly from the memory card in your digital camera to a printer. For those who wish to bypass a computer and image-editing software, it is important to ensure your digital camera and printer are both PictBridge enabled.

RAW: Higher end digital cameras often offer RAW format, which is the highest quality digital picture that can be taken with the camera. Many cameras use their own proprietary RAW formats, and while some manufacturers are working toward a standard for this file format, many find that some RAW files can only be read by certain software programs. Compatibility is still an issue (at the time of printing).

refresh rate: Once you've taken a picture, the time it takes for the camera to be ready to take another picture.

resolution: Resolution indicates the clarity of an image and is used most often to measure quality standards for monitors, printers, scanners, and other graphic equipment. The higher the resolution, the greater detail that can be seen in a picture.

RGB: An additive color system, RGB stands for red, green, and blue, and it is the model that is used for scanners and monitors.

rule of thirds: This is a guideline that helps photographers create the best composition for a photograph. The rule of thirds states that the frame of an image should be divided vertically and horizontally into thirds in order to best position the subject.

SLR: Stands for *single-lens reflex*. Single-lens reflex cameras use a single lens for both viewing and taking the picture. They are sometimes called "through the lens" cameras.

USB: Stands for *universal serial bus*. This is a way to attach peripheral devices such as jump drives and printers so that the computer can "see them" and access them. USB ports are much faster than standard serial bus connections, and many lines of computer technology offer easy-to-access USB ports for connection.

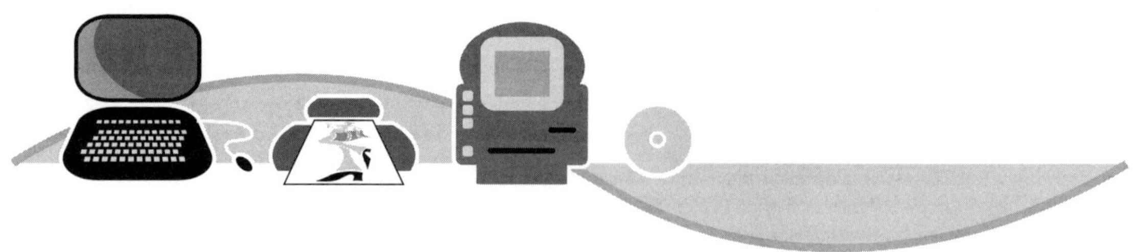

Select Bibliography

Bulkeley, William M. "In Digital Age, a Clash over Fading Photos." *The Wall Street Journal*, April 1, 2005, page B1, E-Commerce/Media section.

Collins, Jim. "Best New Year's Resolution? A Stop Doing List." *USA Today*, December 30, 2003, Editorial/Opinion section.

Covey, Stephen. *The Seven Habits of Highly Effective People, Fifteenth Anniversary Edition*. New York: Free Press, 2004.

Epson America. "Print Permanence." White paper, Epson America, 2005.

Graham, Jefferson. "Digital Camera Boom May Be Nearing Crest." *USA Today*, February 17, 2005, Money section.

Grotta, Daniel, and Sally Wiener Grotta. *PC Magazine Guide to Digital Photography*. Hoboken, NJ: Wiley Publishing, 2004.

Harmon, Amy. "Stop Them Before They Shoot Again." *The New York Times*, May 5, 2005, Styles section.

Lazarus, David. "Precious Photos Disappear." *San Francisco Chronicle*, February 2, 2005.

Mariano, Gwendolyn. "Anatomy of a Photo Failure." *CNET News*, March 20, 2002. http://news.com.com/2008-1082-864900.html?legacy=cnet (accessed summer 2004).

Picture Business. "Imaging Industry to Consumers: Print Those Image Files!" May 2005.

Perenson, Melissa J. "Format Wars Redux: Blu-Ray Disc vs. HD-DVD." *PC World*, February 15, 2005.

Rouvalis, Cristina. "Digital Dilemma: Camera Mistakes and Computer Errors Result in Lost Images." *Pittsburgh Post-Gazette*, June 14, 2005, Interact: Computers & Technology.

Rubin, Ross. "Digital Imaging: The Developing Picture." White paper, NPD Group, January 2005.

Sclobete, Greg. "Lack of Standard Sparks Inkjet Controversy." *TWICE Magazine*, April 4, 2005.

Sheppard, Rob. "Misinformation: What Does Archival Really Mean." *Digital Photo Pro*, May/June 2005.

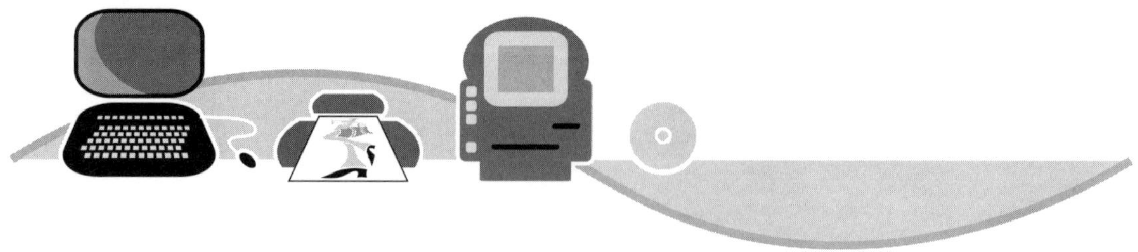

Index

Page numbers in bold type indicate photographs

O

P

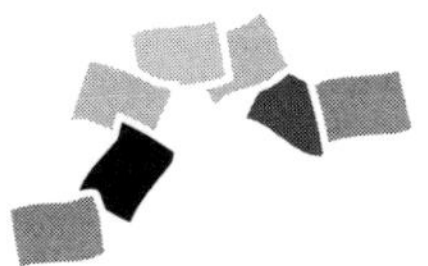

Ordering Information

Compass Trade Press books are available online
and at your favorite bookstore.

Quantity discounts are available to qualifying institutions.
All Compass Trade Press books are available to the booktrade
and educators through all major wholesalers.

For more information visit
www.gotdigitalpictures.com
or contact Laura Oles
laura@gotdigitalpictures.com
Phone: 512-644-8406
Fax: 512-353-2731

Visit www.gotdigitalpictures.com

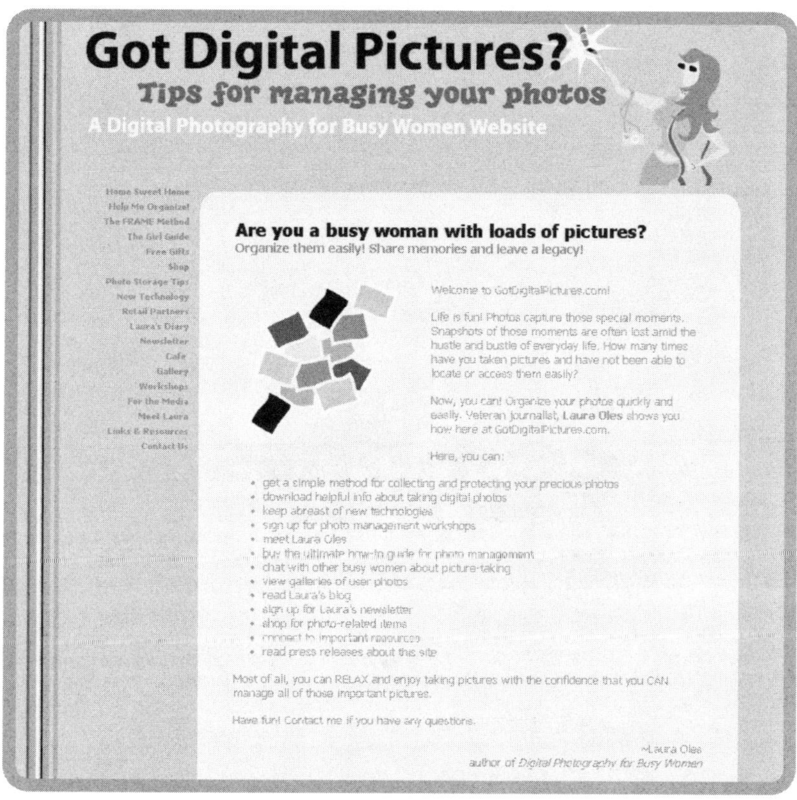

- Download helpful info about taking digital photos
- Keep abreast of new technologies
- Sign up for photo management workshops
- Meet Laura Oles
- Chat with other busy women about picture-taking
- View galleries of user photos
- Read Laura's blog
- Sign up for Laura's newsletter
- Shop for photo-related items
- Connect to important resources

compass
Trade Press